THE GUIDE TO CRAFT BEER

BREWERS
PUBLICATIONS.

Brewers Publications®
A Division of the Brewers Association
PO Box 1679, Boulder, Colorado 80306-1679

BrewersAssociation.org
BrewersPublications.com

. . . .

© Copyright 2019 by Brewers Association

Proudly printed in the United States of America.

. . . .

10 9 8 7 6 5 4 3 2 1
ISBN-13: 978-1-938469-54-1

Library of Congress Cataloging-in-Publication Data

Names: Brewers Publications (Firm)
Title: The guide to craft beer.
Description: Boulder, Colorado : Brewers Publications, a division of the Brewers Association, [2019] | Includes index.
Identifiers: LCCN 2019015899 | ISBN 9781938469541 (pbk.)
Subjects: LCSH: Microbreweries–United States–Guidebooks. | Food and beer pairing.
Classification: LCC TP573.U6 G86 2019 | DDC 641.2/3–dc23
LC record available at https://lccn.loc.gov/2019015899

. . . .

Publisher: Kristi Switzer
Technical Editor: Jess Baker
Contributing Authors: Jess Baker, Julia Herz, Andy Sparhawk, Jay Wood
Copyediting: Iain Cox
Indexing: Doug Easton
Art Direction: Jason Smith
Cover, Interior Design, and Production: Adam Raiola

. . . .

CONTENTS

WHAT IS CRAFT BEER?

NOW IS THE BEST TIME IN US HISTORY TO BE A CRAFT BEER LOVER. BUT WHAT IS CRAFT BEER?

Whether you want to be a craft beer expert or just learn a little more before trying your first craft beer, keep reading. Trying to define craft beer can be perceived as a difficult task, since beer appreciation is very subjective and based upon personal experience. However, the Brewers Association, the not-for-profit trade group that protects and promotes craft brewers in the US, defines an American craft brewer as a "small and independent brewer."

PHOTO © DUSTIN HALL | THE BREWTOGRAPHY PROJECT

As a nation, the US now has more beer styles and brands to choose from than any other market in the world. As of early 2019, more than 7,000 breweries are responsible for the beer brands available in the US. These breweries have had many successes and challenges, but they could not have developed their reputation as producers of the world's best beer without support from beer lovers.

Craft beer is enjoyed during everyday celebrations and is viewed by many as one of life's special pleasures. Each glass displays the creativity and passion of its maker and the complexity of its ingredients. Craft beer is treasured by millions who see it as not merely a fermented beverage, but something to be shared, revered, and enjoyed in moderation.

FUN FACTS

- Craft brewers maintain integrity by what they brew and their general independence, free from a substantial interest by a non-craft brewer.

- Craft brewers are small brewers. Often very small!

- Craft brewers are innovative! Craft brewers interpret historic styles with unique twists and develop new styles that have no precedent.

- Craft beer is generally made with traditional ingredients like malted barley; interesting and sometimes non-traditional ingredients are often added for distinctiveness.

- Craft brewers tend to be very involved in their communities through philanthropy, product donations, volunteerism, and event sponsorship.

- More than 80 percent of adults of legal drinking age in the US live within 10 miles of a brewery.

WHY CRAFT BEER?

SMALL AND INDEPENDENT CRAFT BREWERS HAVE REDEFINED WHAT AMERICAN BEER MEANS.

The phrase "American beer" was once synonymous with a bland, almost commodified product. Today, American beer is thought of as flavorful, experimental, and vast, inspiring even the world's oldest brewing heritages to push their boundaries.

Taste, or more correctly, flavor, is a paramount focus of the American craft beer revolution. However, it is often seen as the only explanation as to why craft beer has become so popular. Small brewers make some incredibly flavorful beers; it is their intention to do so, but flavor is just one element of what makes people connect with craft beer.

Craft beer is about the flavor, but it's so much more— it's an experience.

Visiting an independent brewery, interacting with brewery staff, sampling brews, learning about the brewer's journey, and taking in the brewery's unique experience cannot be recreated by anyone else or anywhere else. The idea for each brewery has a unique story behind it and it is often these stories that engage and cultivate fans.

From breweries born of a sense of place and history to breweries that thematically represent some element of adventure, fun, or sport, breweries are each unique and their brewers are passionate about sharing that with drinkers. Sometimes it is a shared passion for the environment or social justice, while others may share a pride for local culture that cannot be found elsewhere. Building on these relationships and stories—and flavors—helps foster a sense of community and loyalty that reflects the best of these unique gems of American entrepreneurship.

Maybe that's why people find it easier to say craft beer is all about the taste. It's more difficult to adequately explain the wide variety of ways in which dreams come true.

HOW DO I KNOW IF IT'S A CRAFT BEER?

HOW CAN YOU TELL IF A BEER IS MADE BY A US CRAFT BREWER? SEEK THE INDEPENDENT CRAFT BREWER SEAL.

As global beer brands purchase formerly independent craft brewers, knowing which breweries remain independent can be confusing for beer lovers.

Introduced by the Brewers Association (BA) in June 2017, the certification logo is designed as an upside-down beer bottle, which symbolizes how the US craft beer movement has turned beer on its head worldwide. The BA defines a craft brewer as small and independent. Independent brewers in America are not owned by large multinational companies, they are staunchly independent, small, local breweries that participate in their community.

Brewers have been adding the seal to everything tied to their brands, especially packaged beer—bottles, cans, six-pack carriers, case boxes, keg collars, and more.

Join the movement and #SeekTheSeal.

CRAFT
BEER
COMMUNITY

The craft brewing community is about more than beer—it's about the people behind the beer. Small and independent craft breweries are building community with beer lovers, local businesses, and each other. Sustainability, charitable giving, local revitalization, and helping one another are hallmarks of the craft beer industry. It is not uncommon to find brewers helping other brewers with questions or locating a machine part, all to ensure quality beer continues to be produced by other breweries. There have been times when a brewery has needed "just enough" of an ingredient to finish a brew, and has obtained it from another local brewery.

In addition to helping each other out, the brewers are active in the communities where they live and distribute their beers. Craft brewers are well-known for their support of charities, business initiatives, and events that foster pride, support, and connection within their distribution area. It's not just good business, it's also a way for craft brewers to give back to their neighbors, friends, local businesses, and beer lovers.

Some of the ways that craft breweries give back include donating beer, merchandise, or sales proceeds to local charities; building community among homebrewers with special tours, competitions, rallies, or collaborative brewing sessions; innovating to reduce their footprint in communities by working to be more sustainable and environmentally conscious; hiring and training local staff; donating safe spaces for education, discussions, and meetings; and in general being an active member of their communities.

In some areas of the country, craft brewers have led a revitalization of run-down parts of town. The infusion of investment that craft beer brings has paved the way for restaurants, food trucks, and shopping districts. Craft breweries are destinations, and the economic benefits they bring range from additional revenue for city government to increased tourism that benefits many local businesses.

So, when you lift that craft beer to your lips and savor the aroma and flavor, you can feel good about supporting a vibrant and growing community!

DECONSTRUCTING
CRAFT
BEER

PERCEPTION

 Appearance. While flavor is king, a beer's appearance is important. Can anything arouse the senses like a perfectly poured glass of craft beer? Whether it's very pale, gold, amber, copper, brown, or black, craft beer is always aesthetically pleasing. It could be filtered or unfiltered, which affects the clarity or cloudiness of the beer. A thick foam head is a necessary part of the appeal.

 Mouthfeel. The physical sensation of a beer across the tongue and around the inside of the mouth—its mouthfeel—can have a big impact on how the flavors are perceived. The textures one perceives in a beer include carbonation, fullness, and aftertaste.

 Aroma. Even before you drink it, your first whiff of a craft beer sets the stage. Hops, malt, and yeast contribute aromatic qualities by varying degrees. The enticing aromas of bread, fruit, flowers, spice, pine, citrus—and more—prime your senses to enjoy the beverage. The nose knows best!

 Flavor. No drink in the world has craft beer's diverse range of flavors. There are many different styles, each offering a spectrum of tastes to enjoy. Flavors are enhanced as beer warms. Common flavor descriptors include sweet, malty, bitter, bready, spicy, sour, fruity, nutty, roasted, and chocolate.

INGREDIENTS

 Malt. Malt is the soul of beer, as it contributes flavor, aroma, color, and body. Malt is a cereal grain, generally barley, that has been partially germinated then kilned or roasted. During the brewing process, starches are converted into fermentable sugars during a process called mashing. Yeast then feast upon these sugars and produce alcohol and carbon dioxide (CO_2). The types of malt, mash temperatures, and a variety of other factors help determine how the flavors are perceived in beer. Roasted specialty malts impart color and unique flavors like toffee, nuts, chocolate, coffee, bread, raisin, and prune.

Hops. Craft brewers use hops as chefs use spices. The hop plant produces pungent flowers, which are used to add aroma, flavor, and bitterness to beer. Hop bitterness balances malt sweetness and the bittering compounds act as a preservative. Hops are added at various times during brewing and fermentation. There are hundreds of hop varieties, each with their own bittering, flavoring, and aromatic properties.

- **American varieties** – Citrus, fruit, resin, pine
  (Examples: the three "Cs," Cenntennial, Cascade, Chinook)

- **English varieties** – Earthy, herbal
  (Examples: East Kent Goldings, Fuggle)

- **German/noble varieties** – floral, spicy
  (Examples: Hallertau, Spalt, Saaz, Tettnang)

 Yeast. You're not the first one to enjoy the beer in your glass. During fermentation, yeast cells feast on fermentable sugars, expelling alcohol, CO_2, and flavor compounds in the process. The main point of differentiation between types of brewer's yeast is lager versus ale yeast. Within these two broad categories are a wide variety of yeast strains. Some craft brewers make unique beers using a wild yeast called *Brettanomyces*. The yeast may impart distinct flavors to beer, or it can be more neutral. Bottle conditioned craft beer includes live yeast in the packaging, often resulting in a vitamin-rich sediment residing at the bottom of the bottle.

 Water. Terroir is a common term in the wine world, but did you know that local climates and geology affect beer? Depending on the region, water has variable mineral content that contributes to the expression of malt and hops in craft beer. Some water profiles accentuate hop bitterness while others enhance malt flavors. Today, many craft brewers adjust the chemistry of their water to optimize it for the beer styles they produce.

Glassware. Drinking from a bottle is like watching a 3-D movie without the special glasses. Craft beer has amazing flavors if you let them shine. Serve craft beer in a clean, freshly-rinsed glass. Appropriately shaped glassware enhances the aroma, delivers more flavor, and releases bubbles so you ingest less carbonation. Generally, the stronger the beer, the smaller the glass. Beware: frozen glassware causes foaming, masks flavors, and can impart off-flavors.

 Food pairings. Don't tie yourself down with rules when pairing craft beer and food. But, if you're not sure how to begin, certain guidelines can facilitate exploration. Match intensity with intensity. Strong-flavored foods overwhelm light-flavored beers and vice versa. Look for flavor harmonies and bridges between craft beer and food—shared notes that can tie together the pairing. Lastly, create home-run pairings by playing taste elements, like sweet, salty, sour, bitter, and umami, against each other. See page 137 for more ideas for food pairings.

 Serving. Keep it cool. Most lagers of average strength are best enjoyed chilled to 38°F. Many ales and stronger craft beers are enhanced when served closer to cellar temperature, which is 50°F to 55°F. To prevent off-flavors, draught craft beer should be dispensed through well-maintained beer lines that are cleaned every two weeks.

 Savor the flavor responsibly. Your weight, the amount of food in your stomach, the period of time over which you consume craft beer, and other variables determine the rate at which alcohol is absorbed into your bloodstream. Food slows alcohol absorption and can slow your rate of consumption. Don't drive when you've had too much. You already knew that, of course.

BY THE NUMBERS

 SRM: The Standard Reference Method (SRM) refers to a beer's color. A very pale beer, such as American wheat, typically has an SRM of 5, while a dark-colored stout is usually in the range of 25–40 SRM.

 IBU. International bitterness units (IBU) is the measure of the hops' contribution to a beer's bitterness. It can range from zero to over 100. A *weizen* might have 8–15 IBUs, while an India pale ale (IPA) may range from 60–100 IBUs. Beer bitterness is subject to perception. What is aggressively bitter to some is mildly bitter to others. Also, bitterness can seem lower in the presence of residual sugar, carbonation, and cooler temperatures.

 ABV. Alcohol by volume (ABV) varies by craft beer style from around 3% to more than 20%. Alcohol flavor may be perceived, and is sometimes desirable, in craft beers with higher ABV. Craft beer styles in the US average 5.9%.

 Gravity. Gravity refers to the amount of residual sugar in a beer, which often affects mouthfeel. It is expressed in points that are relative to water's gravity, which is 1.000 (i.e., no residual sugar). Fully fermented craft beer gravity averages 1.014 and unfermented craft beer averages 1.060. A higher gravity number indicates that more residual sugar exists in the final product. The potential strength of the beer is tracked by the brewer, who measures the gravity of the wort before and after fermentation, typically using an instrument called a hydrometer.

BEER STYLES

The sheer number of beer styles that make up the craft beer scene is exciting but it can also be intimidating—and that's okay. With all the different beer styles and beer names, however, it is tough to remember what differentiates them from one another.

Craft beer resides at the intersection of art and science. It is up to each individual brewer to decide whether they want to create beer within specific style guidelines or forge a new path and break the mold of traditional styles. Because so many craft brewers brew outside style guidelines, it is impossible to make a list that fully represents the spectrum of beers being created today. This beer style list includes many common styles being made in the US today, but it is not exhaustive.

COMMON US BEER STYLES

Craft brewers use a wide variety of ingredients to achieve the aroma, body, flavor, and finish they desire in their beer. They often take classic, Old World styles from great brewing countries like England, Germany, and Belgium and add their own twists by modifying the amount or type of ingredients or the brewing processes. Due to the popularity of craft beer in America, there are now multiple beer styles uniquely credited to the US.

- California Common
- Imperial IPA
- New England IPA
- American Amber Ale
- American Amber Lager
- American Barleywine
- American Black Ale
- American Brett
- American Brown Ale
- American Cream Ale
- American Imperial Porter
- American Imperial Red
- American Imperial Stout
- American IPA
- American Lager
- American Pale Ale
- American Sour
- American Stout
- American Wheat Wine
- American Wheat

Due to the constant experimentation and exploration by today's US brewers, new beer styles are constantly evolving. That makes it difficult, if not impossible, to fully document all types of beer being made at any given time. Another factor is that new beer styles usually become established by developing a track record of multiple breweries making the same type of beer over years and years. In other words, it takes time before any trendy new type of beer is deemed a recognized beer style.

This style guide has been narrowed down to a list of **81 styles in 15 style families**. Descriptive terms are always listed from least to most intense.

PALE ALE

Pale ale is a catch-all term dating back to the seventeenth century when control of malt color was in its infancy. These beers were simply called "pale" in comparison to the darker beers being produced at the time. Today, these beers are generally produced with two-row malted barley, referred to as pale malt. While more balanced than the hop-forward IPA, some versions of pale ale can push the boundaries of the traditional style.

BEER STYLES

American Pale Ale

Blonde Ale

English-Style Bitter

English-Style Pale Ale (ESB)

American Amber Ale

AMERICAN PALE ALE

While pale ale beer has definitively English roots, many credit Sierra Nevada Brewing Co.'s Pale Ale for the style's current popularity. Sierra Nevada Pale Ale employs the use of American Cascade hops and a clean fermenting ale yeast that has become synonymous with today's West Coast-style craft beers. Characterized by floral, fruity, citrus-like, piney, resinous American hops, the American pale ale is a medium-bodied beer with low to medium caramel malt flavor and carries with it a toasted maltiness.

American pale ale is one of the most food-friendly styles to enjoy, since the pale ale works wonderfully with lighter fare, such as salads and chicken, but can still stand up to a hearty bowl of chili. It can also pair well with a variety of different cheeses, including cheddar, seafood like steamed clams or fish, and even desserts.

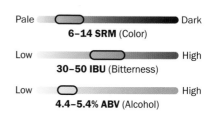

Pale ▬▬▬◖▬▬▬▬▬▬▬ Dark
6–14 SRM (Color)

Low ▬▬▬▬◖▬▬▬▬ High
30–50 IBU (Bitterness)

Low ▬◖▬▬▬▬▬▬▬ High
4.4–5.4% ABV (Alcohol)

OTHER STYLES YOU MAY ENJOY

- American IPA

- Belgian-Style Pale Ale

CATEGORY
PALE ALE

FOOD PAIRINGS

 Roasted or grilled meats

 Mild or medium cheddar

 Apple pie

GLASSWARE & SERVING TEMPERATURE

 Tulip
45–55°F

INGREDIENTS

Hops: Cascade, Centennial

Malt: Pale, caramel, Munich

Yeast: Ale

BLONDE ALE

One of the most approachable styles, a golden or blonde ale is an easy-drinking beer that is visually appealing and has no particularly dominating malt or hop characteristics. Rounded and smooth, it is an American classic known for its simplicity. A blonde ale is sometimes referred to as a "golden ale." These beers can have honey, spices, and fruit added, and may be fermented with lager or ale yeast.

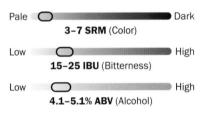

Pale ⬤ Dark
3–7 SRM (Color)

Low ⬤ High
15–25 IBU (Bitterness)

Low ⬤ High
4.1–5.1% ABV (Alcohol)

OTHER STYLES YOU MAY ENJOY

- American Cream Ale
- Berliner-Style Weisse

CATEGORY
PALE ALE

FOOD PAIRINGS

 Spaghetti and meatballs

Pepper Jack

 Sugar cookies

GLASSWARE & SERVING TEMPERATURE

 Tulip
45–50°F

INGREDIENTS

Hops: Willamette

Malt: American two-row, crystal

Yeast: Lager or ale

The English-style bitter is a very sessionable, lower-alcohol, malt-driven style. This broad style description is commonly associated with cask-conditioned beers. The light- to medium-bodied ordinary bitter is gold to copper in color, with a low residual malt sweetness. Hop bitterness is at the brewer's discretion and fruity esters are common.

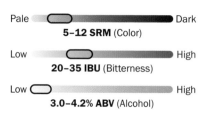

Pale ⬤━━━━━ Dark
5–12 SRM (Color)

Low ━━⬤━━ High
20–35 IBU (Bitterness)

Low ⬤━━━━ High
3.0–4.2% ABV (Alcohol)

OTHER STYLES YOU MAY ENJOY

- Scottish-Style Ale
- Belgian-Style Pale Ale
- Session Beer

CATEGORY
PALE ALE

FOOD PAIRINGS

 Roasted chicken, fish and chips

 Firm English cheeses

 Oatmeal raisin walnut cookies

GLASSWARE & SERVING TEMPERATURE

 Nonic pint
50–55°F

INGREDIENTS

Hops: English varieties

Malt: British pale ale, aromatic, crystal, special roast

Yeast: Ale

ENGLISH-STYLE PALE ALE (ESB)

The designation ESB stands for "extra special bitter." This style is known for its balance and the interplay between malt and hop bitterness. English pale ales display earthy, herbal English-variety hop character. Medium-to-high hop bitterness, flavor, and aroma should be evident. The yeast strains used in this style lend fruity esters to its aromatics and flavor. The residual malt and defining sweetness of this richly flavored, full-bodied bitter is medium to medium-high.

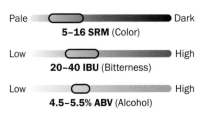

Pale ━━━━ **Dark**
5–16 SRM (Color)

Low ━━━━ **High**
20–40 IBU (Bitterness)

Low ━━━━ **High**
4.5–5.5% ABV (Alcohol)

OTHER STYLES YOU MAY ENJOY

- American Amber Ale
- Scottish-Style Ale
- German-Style Bock

CATEGORY
PALE ALE

FOOD PAIRINGS

 Roasted chicken, fish and chips

 English-style cheeses

 Maple bread pudding

GLASSWARE & SERVING TEMPERATURE

 Nonic pint
50–55°F

INGREDIENTS

Hops: English varieties

Malt: British pale ale, crystal

Yeast: Ale

CATEGORY
PALE ALE

FOOD PAIRINGS

 Barbecue

 Medium cheddar

 Banana pound cake

GLASSWARE & SERVING TEMPERATURE

 Tulip
45–55°F

INGREDIENTS

Hops: Horizon, Cascade, Centennial

Malt: English pale ale or American two-row, crystal, Victory

Yeast: Ale

AMERICAN AMBER ALE

The American amber ale is a cornerstone style of the American craft brewing revolution. American ambers are darker in color than their American pale ale cousins, the presence of caramel and crystal malts lending a toasted, toffee flavor, along with the perception of a fuller body when compared to beers without such malts. Amber ale showcases a medium-high to high malt character with low to medium caramel character derived from the use of roasted crystal malts. The American amber is characterized by American-variety hops, which lend the amber ale notes of citrus, fruit, and pine to balance the sweetness of the malt, making this a highly versatile companion to American cuisine.

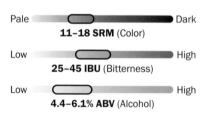

Pale ▬▬▬▬▬▬▬▬▬▬▬ Dark
11–18 SRM (Color)

Low ▬▬▬▬▬▬▬▬▬▬ High
25–45 IBU (Bitterness)

Low ▬▬▬▬▬▬▬▬▬ High
4.4–6.1% ABV (Alcohol)

OTHER STYLES YOU MAY ENJOY

- English-Style Pale Ale
- English-Style Mild
- American Amber Lager

DARK LAGER

The family of malt-accented dark lagers are some of the most accommodating with food pairings. Clean fermenting lager yeast allows the toasted and caramel flavors of dark malts to shine through. Think of dark lagers anytime you are grilling meat and vegetables, as they offer a straightforward complement to the roasty elements of grilled food.

BEER STYLES

American Amber Lager

German-Style Dunkel

German-Style Märzen /
Oktoberfest

German-Style Schwarzbier

Vienna-Style Lager

AMERICAN AMBER LAGER

American amber lager is a widely available, sessionable craft beer style that showcases both malt and hops. Amber lagers are a medium-bodied lager with a toasty or caramel-like malt character. Hop bitterness can range from very low to medium-high.

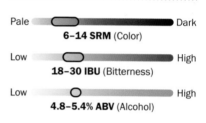

Pale ▬▬▬▬▬▬▬ Dark
6–14 SRM (Color)

Low ▬▬▬▬▬▬▬ High
18–30 IBU (Bitterness)

Low ▬▬▬▬▬▬▬ High
4.8–5.4% ABV (Alcohol)

OTHER STYLES YOU MAY ENJOY

- German-Style Oktoberfest
- Vienna-Style Lager
- English-Style Mild

GERMAN-STYLE DUNKEL

The German-style *dunkel* (German for "dark") is a lager-style beer. It offers beer lovers balanced flavors of chocolate, bread crust, and caramel from the use of Munich malt. Despite the malt-forward flavor profile, this beer does not offer an overly sweet impression. Rather, you'll find a delicate balance between the distinct character of malt and the refined touch of bitterness from noble hops, indicative of what many beer drinkers expect from German beer styles. Like most German beers, dunkel beer is a great candidate for food pairing, matching up well to grilled meats.

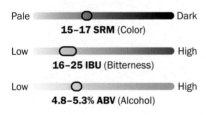

Pale ●——————————— Dark
15–17 SRM (Color)

Low ●——————————— High
16–25 IBU (Bitterness)

Low ●——————————— High
4.8–5.3% ABV (Alcohol)

OTHER STYLES YOU MAY ENJOY
- Belgian-Style Dubbel
- English-Style Brown Porter

GERMAN-STYLE MÄRZEN / OKTOBERFEST

German-style Märzen is a beer rich in malt with a balance of clean hop bitterness. Bread or biscuit-like malt aroma and flavor is common. Originating in Germany, this style used to be seasonally available in the spring (*Märzen* meaning "March"), with the festival-style versions tapped in October, hence Oktoberfest.

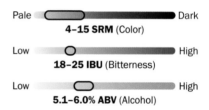

Pale ▭▭▭▭▭ Dark
4–15 SRM (Color)

Low ▭▭▭▭▭ High
18–25 IBU (Bitterness)

Low ▭▭▭▭▭ High
5.1–6.0% ABV (Alcohol)

OTHER STYLES YOU MAY ENJOY

- English-Style Brown Ale
- Belgian-Style Pale Ale
- American Amber Lager

GERMAN-STYLE SCHWARZBIER

While sometimes called black lager because it may remind some of German-style dunkel, *schwarzbier* is a drier, darker and more roast-oriented beer. These very dark brown to black beers have a surprisingly light-colored foam head (not excessively brown) with good cling quality. Schwarzbiers have a mild roasted malt character without the associated bitterness. Malt flavor and aroma is at low to medium levels of sweetness.

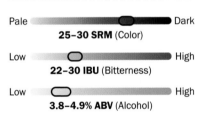

Pale   Dark
25–30 SRM (Color)

Low   High
22–30 IBU (Bitterness)

Low   High
3.8–4.9% ABV (Alcohol)

OTHER STYLES YOU MAY ENJOY

- Irish-Style Dry Stout

- Belgian-Style Dubbel

VIENNA-STYLE LAGER

Vienna-style lager ranges from copper to reddish brown in color. The beer is characterized by a malty aroma and slight malt sweetness. The malt aroma and flavor should have a notable degree of toasted and/or slightly roasted malt character. Hop bitterness is low to medium-low.

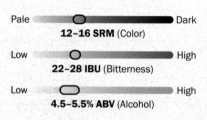

Pale ⬤ Dark
12–16 SRM (Color)

Low ⬤ High
22–28 IBU (Bitterness)

Low ⬤ High
4.5–5.5% ABV (Alcohol)

OTHER STYLES YOU MAY ENJOY

- German-Style Bock
- Belgian-Style Dubbel

BROWN ALE

Amber to brown in color, this beer family exhibits a light nutty maltiness with hints of toast. They tend to be crisp to medium-bodied and are usually lightly hopped. A great style to pair with braised or grilled meat and aged cheese, or enjoy just on its own.

BEER STYLES

American Brown Ale

English-Style Brown Ale

English-Style Mild Ale

AMERICAN BROWN ALE

For American brown ale, roasted malt, caramel-like, and chocolate-like characters should be of medium intensity in both the flavor and aroma. American brown ales have evident low to medium hop flavor and aroma and medium to high hop bitterness. The history of this style dates back to US homebrewers who were inspired by English brown ales and porters. Its flavor sits somewhere between those English styles and is more bitter than both.

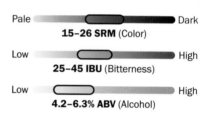

Pale ⸺⸺⸺⸺⸺⸺⸺⸺ Dark
15–26 SRM (Color)

Low ⸺⸺⸺⸺⸺⸺⸺⸺ High
25–45 IBU (Bitterness)

Low ⸺⸺⸺⸺⸺⸺⸺⸺ High
4.2–6.3% ABV (Alcohol)

OTHER STYLES YOU MAY ENJOY

- Scottish-Style Ale

- Vienna-Style Lager

- Fruit and Field Beer

ENGLISH-STYLE BROWN ALE

A bona fide English beer classic, the English brown ale is easily one of the most iconic beer styles. Toasty, robust, and with a bit of chocolate maltiness, English-style brown ale is neither flashy nor boring. English-style brown ales have two variations: a dry, roasted version that is said to have originated from northern England, and a sweeter, less attenuated brown ale variety that is believed to have been more popular in southern England. Both offer a toasted nut, chocolatey character indicative of brown ales. They will not be as hoppy or bitter as their American counterparts and favor English hops as well as characterful English ale yeast.

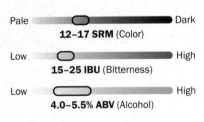

Pale ▬▬▬○▬▬▬ Dark
12–17 SRM (Color)

Low ▬○▬▬▬▬▬ High
15–25 IBU (Bitterness)

Low ▬○▬▬▬▬▬ High
4.0–5.5% ABV (Alcohol)

OTHER STYLES YOU MAY ENJOY

- Belgian-Style Dubbel

- English-Style Mild

- Germany-Style Dunkel

CATEGORY
BROWN ALE

FOOD PAIRINGS

 Roasted pork, steak, nuts

 Aged Gouda

 Pear fritters

GLASSWARE & SERVING TEMPERATURE

Nonic pint
50–55°F

INGREDIENTS

Hops: English varieties (e.g. East Kent Goldings, Fuggle)

Malt: Pale ale, Victory, crystal, pale chocolate

Yeast: Ale

Malt and caramel are part of the flavor and aroma profile of the English-style mild, while licorice and roast malt tones may sometimes contribute as well. Hop bitterness is very low to low. American brewers are known to make lighter-colored versions as well as the more common "dark mild." These beers are very low in alcohol, yet retain a medium body.

CATEGORY
BROWN ALE

FOOD PAIRINGS

 Mushrooms and wild game

 Mild cheddar

 Dark fruit tart

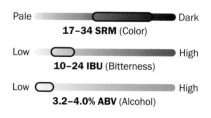

Pale ▬▬▬▬▬▬▬ Dark
17–34 SRM (Color)

Low ▬▬▬▬▬▬▬ High
10–24 IBU (Bitterness)

Low ▬▬▬▬▬▬▬ High
3.2–4.0% ABV (Alcohol)

GLASSWARE & SERVING TEMPERATURE

 Nonic pint
50–55°F

OTHER STYLES YOU MAY ENJOY

- Belgian-Style Pale Ale
- American Amber Lager

INGREDIENTS

Hops: English varieties

Malt: British pale ale, crystal, pale chocolate, black patent

Yeast: Ale

INDIA PALE ALE

An extension of the pale ale category with higher gravity ranges and an enhanced hop presence, India pale ale (IPA) has become one of the most popular styles of beer in the craft beer world. English and American examples differ due to the ingredients used, particularly the hop varieties. Although malt flavors are often present and offer balance, IPAs are a true celebration of hop aroma, flavor, and bitterness. Newly developed hop varieties continue to bring exciting flavors to this style, proving that bitter is beautiful.

BEER STYLES

American IPA

English-Style IPA

Imperial IPA

New England IPA

Characterized by floral, fruity, citrus-like, piney or resinous American-variety hop character, the IPA beer style is all about hop flavor, aroma, and bitterness. This has been the one of the most-entered categories at the Great American Beer Festival® for more than a decade, and is the top-selling craft beer style in supermarkets and liquor stores across the US.

CATEGORY
INDIA PALE ALE

FOOD PAIRINGS

 Spicy tuna roll

 Blue cheeses

 Persimmon rice pudding

GLASSWARE & SERVING TEMPERATURE

 Tulip
50–55°F

INGREDIENTS

Hops: Centennial, Simcoe, Amarillo

Malt: American two-row

Yeast: Ale

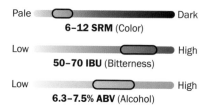

Pale ▬▬▬▬▬▬▬▬▬▬ Dark
6–12 SRM (Color)

Low ▬▬▬▬▬▬▬▬▬▬ High
50–70 IBU (Bitterness)

Low ▬▬▬▬▬▬▬▬▬▬ High
6.3–7.5% ABV (Alcohol)

OTHER STYLES YOU MAY ENJOY
- American Black Ale
- German-Style Pilsner

ENGLISH-STYLE IPA

Steeped in lore (and extra hops), the English-style IPA is a stronger version of a pale ale. Characterized by a hearty helping of English hop character (earthy, floral) and increased alcohol content, English yeast lend a fruity character to the flavor and aroma. The English version strikes a balance between malt and hops for a more rounded flavor.

There is also a lot of mythology surrounding the creation of this style, which is still debated today. Beers similar to what made the trip to India had been in production for domestic consumption prior to any reports of it being exported. Records show that other beer styles, including porter, made their way to British India and were enjoyed by parched soldiers and colonists.

CATEGORY
INDIA PALE ALE

FOOD PAIRINGS

 Fettuccine alfredo

 Aged cheddar

 Ginger spice cake

. . . .

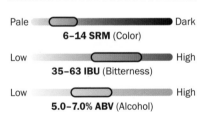

Pale ▬▬▬▬▬▬▬▬▬▬▬▬▬ Dark
6–14 SRM (Color)

Low ▬▬▬▬▬▬▬▬▬▬▬▬▬ High
35–63 IBU (Bitterness)

Low ▬▬▬▬▬▬▬▬▬▬▬▬▬ High
5.0–7.0% ABV (Alcohol)

. . . .

OTHER STYLES YOU MAY ENJOY

- Belgian-Style Pale Ale
- German-Style Märzen/Oktoberfest
- American Amber Ale

GLASSWARE & SERVING TEMPERATURE

Nonic Pint
45–50°F

INGREDIENTS

Hops: Varies, but usually British varieties

Malt: British pale ale, biscuit, crystal

Yeast: Ale

IMPERIAL IPA

A stronger version of American IPA, the imperial IPA beer style creeps toward some of the strongest ales available in terms of alcohol content. Imperial IPA is darker in color than American IPA, substantially more bitter, and high in alcohol by volume. Hop flavor and aroma is fresh, lively, not harsh, and derived from any variety of hops. Alcohol content is medium-high to high and notably evident with a medium-high to full body.

CATEGORY
INDIA PALE ALE

FOOD PAIRINGS

 Bone-in pork chops, miso salmon

 Rich cheeses

 Carrot cake

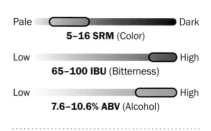

Pale ▬▬▬▬▬▬▬ Dark
5–16 SRM (Color)

Low ▬▬▬▬▬▬▬ High
65–100 IBU (Bitterness)

Low ▬▬▬▬▬▬▬ High
7.6–10.6% ABV (Alcohol)

OTHER STYLES YOU MAY ENJOY
- American Black Ale

GLASSWARE & SERVING TEMPERATURE

 Tulip
50–55°F

INGREDIENTS

Hops: Varies

Malt: American two-row, crystal, malted wheat

Yeast: Ale

NEW ENGLAND IPA

Emphasizing hop aroma and flavor without bracing bitterness, the New England IPA leans heavily on late and dry-hopping techniques to deliver a beer bursting with juicy, tropical hop flavor. The skillful balance of technique and ingredient selection, often including the addition of wheat or oats, lends an alluring haze to this popular take on the American IPA.

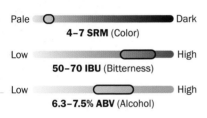

Pale ⬤ Dark
4–7 SRM (Color)

Low High
50–70 IBU (Bitterness)

Low High
6.3–7.5% ABV (Alcohol)

OTHER STYLES YOU MAY ENJOY

- American Black Ale
- German-Style Hefeweizen
- Contemporary Gose

CATEGORY
INDIA PALE ALE

FOOD PAIRINGS

 Hawaiian pork tenderloin

 Goat blue

 Macha creme brulee

GLASSWARE & SERVING TEMPERATURE

 Nonic Pint
45–55°F

INGREDIENTS

Hops: US hops

Malt: A variety of British and American base malts can be used

Yeast: Ale

WHEAT BEER

Typically, 40–60 percent of the grains used in wheat beers are wheat. Wheat adds a creamy, slightly tangy flavor to these styles. With wheat as the common denominator, these beers differ in flavor and aroma due to the particular types of yeast used and, in the case of Belgian-style *witbier*, the addition of other ingredients like coriander and orange peel.

BEER STYLES

American-Style Wheat Wine Ale	Berliner-Style Weisse
American Wheat	German-Style Dunkelweizen
Belgian-Style Witbier	German-Style Hefeweizen

AMERICAN-STYLE WHEAT WINE ALE

Part of the "strong ale" category, American-style wheat wine ale is not derived from grapes as its name might suggest. Made with at least 50 percent wheat malt, this full-bodied beer features bready and candy flavors, and finishes with a great deal of malty sweetness. These beers may be oak-aged and sometimes have small amounts of darker malts added. The fruity ester aroma is often high and counterbalanced by a complex alcohol character.

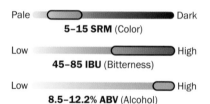

Pale ⬤━━━━━━ Dark
5–15 SRM (Color)

Low ━━━━⬤ High
45–85 IBU (Bitterness)

Low ━━━━━⬤ High
8.5–12.2% ABV (Alcohol)

OTHER STYLES YOU MAY ENJOY
- German-Style Dunkelweizen
- Belgian-Style Blonde Ale
- Belgian-Style Tripel

CATEGORY
WHEAT BEER

FOOD PAIRINGS

 Smoked trout

 Asiago

 Peach sorbet

GLASSWARE & SERVING TEMPERATURE

 Snifter
50–55°F

INGREDIENTS

Hops: Varies

Malt: At least 50% malted wheat

Yeast: Ale

AMERICAN WHEAT

American wheat beers are some of the most approachable beers in the craft beer world. Brewed with at least 30 percent malted wheat, this style can be made with either ale or lager yeast. Like the traditional German *hefeweizen*, these beers are often served unfiltered and can have a cloudy appearance when roused. Hoppier American wheat beers differ from their German cousins in that they don't offer the flavors of banana or clove derived from the weizen yeast strain. The American wheat's composition is accepting of additional ingredients, particularly raspberries, watermelon, and even chili peppers.

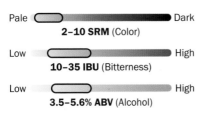

Pale ▢ Dark
2–10 SRM (Color)

Low ▢ High
10–35 IBU (Bitterness)

Low ▢ High
3.5–5.6% ABV (Alcohol)

OTHER STYLES YOU MAY ENJOY

- Belgian-Style Tripel
- Fruit and Field Beer

BELGIAN-STYLE WITBIER

Belgian-style witbier is brewed using unmalted wheat, sometimes oats and malted barley. Witbiers are spiced with coriander and orange peel. A style that dates back hundreds of years, it fell into relative obscurity until it was revived by Belgian brewer Pierre Celis in the 1960s. This style is currently enjoying a renaissance, especially in the American market. Unfiltered starch and yeast haze should be part of the appearance. These beers were called *wit,* literally "white," due to their hazy appearance.

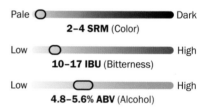

Pale ◯ Dark
2–4 SRM (Color)

Low ◯ High
10–17 IBU (Bitterness)

Low ◯ High
4.8–5.6% ABV (Alcohol)

OTHER STYLES YOU MAY ENJOY

- Bohemian-Style Pilsner
- Fruit and Field Beer
- German-Style Hefeweizen

BERLINER-STYLE WEISSE

Low in alcohol, refreshingly tart, and often served with a flavored syrup like woodruff or raspberry, the Berliner-style *weisse* presents a harmony between yeast and lactic acid. These beers are very pale in color and may be cloudy as they are often unfiltered. Hops are not a feature, but these beers do traditionally showcase esters produced by *Brettanomyces* yeast. Growing in popularity in the US, brewers are adding traditional and exotic fruits to the recipe, resulting in beers with flavorful finishes and striking, colorful hues. Bitterness, alcohol, and residual sugar are very low, allowing the beer's acidity, white bread, and graham cracker malt flavors to shine. Carbonation is very high, adding to the refreshment factor this style delivers. Many examples of this style contain no hops and thus have no bitterness at all.

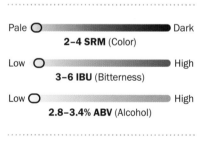

Pale ◯▬▬▬▬ Dark
2–4 SRM (Color)

Low ◯▬▬▬▬ High
3–6 IBU (Bitterness)

Low ◯▬▬▬▬ High
2.8–3.4% ABV (Alcohol)

OTHER STYLES YOU MAY ENJOY

- Belgian-Style Witbier
- American Sour
- American Wheat

CATEGORY
WHEAT BEER

FOOD PAIRINGS

 Aged ham on pretzel bread

 Havarti

 Cheesecake w/ raspberries

GLASSWARE & SERVING TEMPERATURE

Goblet
45–50°F

INGREDIENTS

Hops: German noble (Hallertau, Spalt, Saaz, Tettnang)

Malt: Pilsner, malted wheat

Yeast: Lager or Ale

GERMAN-STYLE DUNKELWEIZEN

The German-style *dunkelweizen* can be considered a cross between a German-style dunkel and a hefeweizen. Distinguished by its sweet maltiness and chocolate-like character, dunkelweizen can also have banana and clove (and occasionally vanilla or bubblegum) esters from the weizen ale yeast.

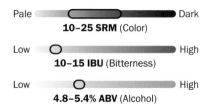

Pale ▬▬▬▬▬▬ Dark
10–25 SRM (Color)

Low ▬▬▬▬▬▬ High
10–15 IBU (Bitterness)

Low ▬▬▬▬▬▬ High
4.8–5.4% ABV (Alcohol)

OTHER STYLES YOU MAY ENJOY
- English-Style Brown Ale
- Baltic-Style Porter

CATEGORY
WHEAT BEER

FOOD PAIRINGS

 Roasted chicken

 Gouda

 Banana cream pie

GLASSWARE & SERVING TEMPERATURE

 Vase
45–50°F

INGREDIENTS

Hops: German noble

Malt: At least 50% malted wheat

Yeast: Weizen ale

GERMAN-STYLE HEFEWEIZEN

In German, *hefe* refers to the yeast that remains in suspension, giving this German beer its cloudy appearance, and *weizen* denotes the use of wheat. German-style wheat beer is at its best when poured into a weizen vase, a large curvaceous glass that showcases the beer's beautiful glow and corrals its large, persistent foam cap produced by the style's characteristic effervescence. A German-style *weissbier* ("white beer") must showcase the weizen yeast's one-two punch of fruit and spice for it to be recognized as a proper German-style hefeweizen. The bright fruitiness of banana alongside the pungency of clove allow this beer to work well with a variety of lighter foods, such as salads, seafood, and a variety of egg dishes.

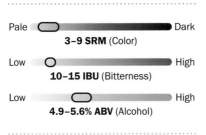

Pale ⬤━━━━━━━ Dark
3–9 SRM (Color)

Low ○━━━━━━━ High
10–15 IBU (Bitterness)

Low ━━━⬤━━━━ High
4.9–5.6% ABV (Alcohol)

OTHER STYLES YOU MAY ENJOY

- Belgian-Style Witbier
- American IPA

CATEGORY
WHEAT BEER

FOOD PAIRINGS

 Seafood

 Chèvre

 Key lime pie

GLASSWARE & SERVING TEMPERATURE

 Vase
40–45°F

INGREDIENTS

Hops: German noble (Hallertau, Spalt, Saaz, Tettnang)

Malt: Pilsner, malted wheat

Yeast: Weizen ale

STRONG ALE

Varying in strength, color, and hop character, strong ales are rich, fuller-bodied, and meant for sipping. Strong ales start off with a relatively large amount of fermentable sugars for yeast to consume. The result is a beer with alcohol content stronger than that of other beer styles.

BEER STYLES

American Barleywine

American Imperial Red Ale

British-Style Barleywine

English-Style Old Ale

American barleywine ranges from amber to deep red/copper-garnet in color. A caramel and/or toffee aroma and flavor are often part of the malt character, along with high residual malty sweetness. Alcohol complexity is evident and fruity ester levels are often high. As with many American versions of a style, American barleywine is typically more hop-forward and bitter than its British counterpart. Low levels of age-induced oxidation can harmonize with other flavors and enhance the overall experience.

CATEGORY
STRONG ALE

FOOD PAIRINGS

 Beef cheek

 Strong blue cheeses

 Rich desserts

GLASSWARE & SERVING TEMPERATURE

 Snifter
50–55°F

INGREDIENTS

Hops: Magnum, Chinook, Centennial, Amarillo

Malt: Pale, crystal, pale chocolate, Special "B"

Yeast: Ale

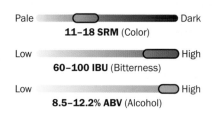

Pale ⬤ Dark
11–18 SRM (Color)

Low ⬤ High
60–100 IBU (Bitterness)

Low ⬤ High
8.5–12.2% ABV (Alcohol)

OTHER STYLES YOU MAY ENJOY
- Imperial India Pale Ale
- German-Style Doppelbock
- Scotch Ale/Wee Heavy

AMERICAN IMPERIAL RED ALE

The use of American hops in the American imperial red ale lends a perception of medium hop bitterness, flavor, and aroma. Coupled with a solid malt profile, this should be a beer balanced between hop bitterness and malt sweetness. This is another example of modern American brewers taking an established style and boosting the flavor. California brewers are credited with creating this innovative style.

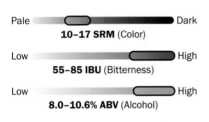

Pale ●━━━━━━ Dark
10–17 SRM (Color)

Low ━━━━━●━ High
55–85 IBU (Bitterness)

Low ━━━━●━ High
8.0–10.6% ABV (Alcohol)

OTHER STYLES YOU MAY ENJOY
- Vienna-Style Lager
- Belgian-Style Quadrupel

BRITISH-STYLE BARLEYWINE

The designation "British-style barleywine" represents a group of strong ales that rival the strength and complexity of some of the world's most celebrated beverages. This brawny, malt-forward beer style is often one of the strongest beer styles on any given beer menu, and showcases a complex mélange of toffee and fruit flavors counterbalanced by warming alcohol and sturdy hop bitterness. With a wide color range and characteristically high alcohol content, this is a style that is often aged, and it evolves well over time. Barleywine shares wine's compatibility with food, favoring rich dishes, desserts, the strongest of cheeses, and even makes for a great digestif.

CATEGORY
STRONG ALE

FOOD PAIRINGS

 Moroccan duck

 Stilton

 Dark chocolate

GLASSWARE & SERVING
TEMPERATURE

Snifter
50–55°F

INGREDIENTS

Hops: English varieties (e.g. East Kent Goldings, Horizon)

Malt: English pale ale, Caramunich®, crystal

Yeast: Ale

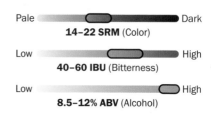

Pale ——————————— Dark
14–22 SRM (Color)

Low ——————————— High
40–60 IBU (Bitterness)

Low ——————————— High
8.5–12% ABV (Alcohol)

OTHER STYLES YOU MAY ENJOY
• English-Style Old Ale

ENGLISH-STYLE OLD ALE

A distinctive quality of English-style old ales is that their yeast undergoes an aging process (often for years) in bulk storage or through bottle conditioning, which contributes to a rich, wine-like, and often sweet oxidation character. Old ales are copper-red to very dark in color. A complex estery character may emerge.

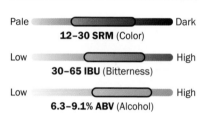

Pale ▬▬▬▬▬▬▬▬ Dark
12–30 SRM (Color)

Low ▬▬▬▬▬▬▬▬ High
30–65 IBU (Bitterness)

Low ▬▬▬▬▬▬▬▬ High
6.3–9.1% ABV (Alcohol)

OTHER STYLES YOU MAY ENJOY

- Belgian-Style Golden Strong Ale
- German-Style Doppelbock
- Belgian-Style Quadrupel

CATEGORY
STRONG ALE

FOOD PAIRINGS

 Roast beef and lamb

 Double Gloucester

 Spiced plum walnut tart

GLASSWARE & SERVING TEMPERATURE

 Snifter
50–55°F

INGREDIENTS

Hops: English varieties

Malt: Pale ale, chocolate, black patent

Yeast: Ale, possibly *Brettanomyces*

BELGIAN STYLES

Belgian-style ales offer unique flavors that make for a highly enjoyable experience. Generally speaking, it is the particular yeast used that contributes the fruit and spice characteristics commonly associated with Belgian-style ales. Some styles in this group may receive the addition of Belgian candi sugar that can be noticeable in the ale's character.

BEER STYLES

Belgian-Style Blonde Ale

Belgian-Style Dubbel

Belgian-Style Golden Strong Ale

Belgian-Style Pale Ale

Belgian-Style Quadrupel

Belgian-Style Saison

Belgian-Style Tripel

CATEGORY
BELGIAN STYLES

FOOD PAIRINGS

 Sweet and sour
chicken

 Brie

 Angel food cake

GLASSWARE & SERVING
TEMPERATURE

Tulip
40–50°F

INGREDIENTS

Hops: Hallertau

Malt: Pilsner, malted
wheat, aromatic

Yeast: Ale

BELGIAN-STYLE BLONDE ALE

Belgian-style blonde ale is typically easy-drinking, with a low but pleasing hop bitterness. This is a light- to medium-bodied ale, with a low malt aroma that has a spiced and sometimes fruity-ester character. Sugar is sometimes added to lighten the perceived body. This style is medium in sweetness and not as bitter as a Belgian-style *tripel* or golden strong ale. Belgian-style blonde ales are usually brilliantly clear. The overall impression is balance between light sweetness, spice, and low to medium fruity ester flavors.

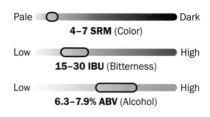

Pale ●━━━━━━ Dark
4–7 SRM (Color)

Low ━━●━━━ High
15–30 IBU (Bitterness)

Low ━━━━●━ High
6.3–7.9% ABV (Alcohol)

OTHER STYLES YOU MAY ENJOY

- German-Style Pilsner
- American Cream Ale

BELGIAN-STYLE DUBBEL

The Belgian-style *dubbel* ranges from brown to very dark in color. Beers in this style have a malty sweetness, which can include cocoa and caramel aromas and flavors. Hop bitterness is medium-low to medium. Yeast-derived fruity esters can be apparent. Often bottle conditioned, a slight yeast haze and flavor may be evident. *Dubbel* meaning "double," this beer is still not so big in intensity as to surpass the Belgian-style quadrupel that is often considered its sibling.

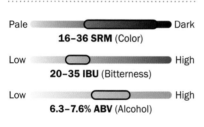

Pale ▬▬▬▬▬▬▬▬▬ Dark
16–36 SRM (Color)

Low ▬▬▬▬▬▬▬▬▬ High
20–35 IBU (Bitterness)

Low ▬▬▬▬▬▬▬▬▬ High
6.3–7.6% ABV (Alcohol)

OTHER STYLES YOU MAY ENJOY

- English-Style Brown Porter
- German-Style Dunkel
- Fruit and Field Beer

CATEGORY
BELGIAN STYLES

FOOD PAIRINGS

 Apple-smoked sausage

 Washed-rind cheeses

 Milk chocolate

GLASSWARE & SERVING TEMPERATURE

 Tulip
50–55°F

INGREDIENTS

Hops: Tettnang

Malt: Pilsner, Caramunich, Special "B"

Yeast: Ale

BELGIAN-STYLE GOLDEN STRONG ALE

The Belgian-style golden strong ale is fruity, complex, and on the higher end of the alcohol spectrum, yet these beers are approachable to many different palates. Look for a characteristic spiciness from Belgian yeast and a dry finish. This style is traditionally drier and lighter in color than a Belgian-style tripel.

CATEGORY
BELGIAN STYLES

FOOD PAIRINGS

 Beer-battered fried shrimp

 Brie

 Baklava

GLASSWARE & SERVING TEMPERATURE

 Tulip
40–45°F

INGREDIENTS

Hops: Tettnang

Malt: Pilsner, Caramunich, Special "B"

Yeast: Ale

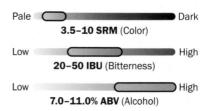

Pale ▭ Dark
3.5–10 SRM (Color)

Low ▭ High
20–50 IBU (Bitterness)

Low ▭ High
7.0–11.0% ABV (Alcohol)

OTHER STYLES YOU MAY ENJOY

- American Wheat
- German-Style Bock

BELGIAN-STYLE PALE ALE

The Belgian-style pale ale is gold to copper in color and can have caramel or toasted malt flavor. The style is characterized by low but noticeable hop bitterness, flavor, and aroma. Fruity esters or spiciness might be present in the flavor or aroma. These beers were inspired by British pale ales.

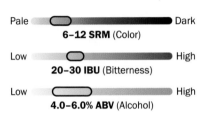

Pale ▬▬▬▬▬▬▬▬▬ Dark
6–12 SRM (Color)

Low ▬▬▬▬▬▬▬▬▬ High
20–30 IBU (Bitterness)

Low ▬▬▬▬▬▬▬▬▬ High
4.0–6.0% ABV (Alcohol)

OTHER STYLES YOU MAY ENJOY

- English-Style Brown Ale
- American Amber Ale
- Vienna-Style Lager

BELGIAN-STYLE QUADRUPEL

The Belgian-style *quadrupel* is amber to dark brown in color. Caramel, dark sugar, and malty sweet flavors dominate, with medium-low to medium-high hop bitterness. "Quads" have a relatively light body compared to their alcoholic strength. Complex fruity flavors emerge, reminiscent of raisins, dates, figs, grapes and/or plums, which are often accompanied by a hint of wine-like character. If aged, oxidative qualities (plum, sherry, stone fruit aromas/flavors) should be mild and not distracting. Beers in this style are sometimes referred to as Belgian strong dark. Caramel, dark sugar, and malty sweet flavors and aromas can be intense, but not cloying, and should complement the fruitiness.

CATEGORY
BELGIAN STYLES

FOOD PAIRINGS

 Roasted duck

 Aged Gouda

 Bread pudding

GLASSWARE & SERVING TEMPERATURE

 Tulip
50–55°F

INGREDIENTS

Hops: Varies

Malt: Varies

Yeast: Ale

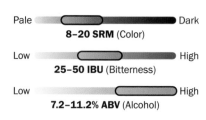

Pale		Dark
8–20 SRM (Color)		

Low		High
25–50 IBU (Bitterness)		

Low		High
7.2–11.2% ABV (Alcohol)		

OTHER STYLES YOU MAY ENJOY

- Barleywine

- Imperial Stout

- German-Style Doppelbock

BELGIAN-STYLE SAISON

Belgian-style saisons are often bottle-conditioned, resulting in some yeast character and high carbonation. Commonly called "farmhouse ales" and originating as summertime beers in Belgium, these are not just warm-weather treats. American craft brewers brew them year-round and have taken to adding a variety of additional ingredients. Belgian-style saisons may have a *Brettanomyces* or lactic acid character, and fruity, horsey, goaty and/or leather-like aromas and flavors. Specialty ingredients, including spices, may contribute a unique and signature character. Malt flavor is low but provides a foundation for the overall balance.

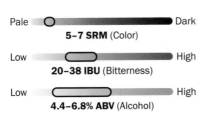

Pale ⬤━━━━━━━ Dark
5–7 SRM (Color)

Low ━━⬤━━━━ High
20–38 IBU (Bitterness)

Low ━⬤━━━━━ High
4.4–6.8% ABV (Alcohol)

OTHER STYLES YOU MAY ENJOY

- American Pale Ale
- German-Style Pilsner
- Session Beer

CATEGORY
BELGIAN STYLES

FOOD PAIRINGS

 Seafood (mussels)

 Brie

 Lemon ginger sorbet

GLASSWARE & SERVING TEMPERATURE

Tulip
45–55°F

INGREDIENTS

Hops: German/noble, English

Malt: Pilsner, Munich, malted wheat

Yeast: Ale, possibly *Brettanomyces*

BELGIAN-STYLE TRIPEL

A Belgian-style tripel is often at the higher end of the alcohol spectrum, yet is still approachable to many different palates. A complex, sometimes mild spicy flavor characterizes this style. Yeast-driven complexity is common. Clove-like phenolic flavor may be evident at very low levels and fruity esters (banana, orange) can be present. These beers are commonly bottle conditioned and finish dry. They may exhibit a slight yeast haze, but the yeast should not be intentionally roused. Belgian-style tripels are similar to Belgian-style golden strong ales, but are generally darker and have a more noticeable malt sweetness.

CATEGORY
BELGIAN STYLES

FOOD PAIRINGS

 Roasted turkey

 Triple creme

 Caramelized banana crème brûlée

GLASSWARE & SERVING TEMPERATURE

 Tulip
40–45°F

INGREDIENTS

Hops: Tettnang, Czech Saaz

Malt: Belgian Pilsner

Yeast: Ale

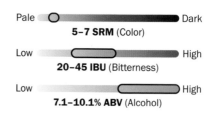

Pale ⬤ Dark
5–7 SRM (Color)

Low ⬤ High
20–45 IBU (Bitterness)

Low ⬤ High
7.1–10.1% ABV (Alcohol)

OTHER STYLES YOU MAY ENJOY

- Imperial India Pale Ale

- Barrel-Aged Beer

- German-Style Maibock

HYBRID BEERS

Light and refreshing, ale-lager hybrid beers are perfect for warm summer days and have become a style favored by American craft brewers and beer lovers alike. In addition to their thirst-quenching ability, they also are a fun beer to enjoy with food, including traditional German sausages and sauerkraut.

BEER STYLES

American Cream Ale	German-Style Altbier
French-Style Bière de Garde	German-Style Kölsch
California Common	Irish-Style Red Ale

AMERICAN CREAM ALE

American cream ale is a mild, pale, light-bodied ale, made using a warm fermentation (top or bottom fermenting yeast) that is followed by cold lagering. Despite being called an ale, it is not uncommon for brewers to use lager yeast instead of ale yeast. Hop aroma is usually absent, and hop flavor and bitterness is very low to low. While the flavor of many traditional German-style lagers contains noticeable sulfur characteristics from the fermentation, this character should be extremely low or absent from cream ales. Any perceptible buttery flavor—reminiscent of microwave popcorn—should be considered a flaw. The buttery flavor is due to a compound called diacetyl, which is normally broken down by the yeast in a long, healthy fermentation.

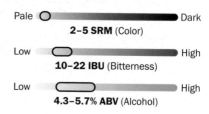

Pale ⬤ Dark
2–5 SRM (Color)

Low ⬤ High
10–22 IBU (Bitterness)

Low ⬤ High
4.3–5.7% ABV (Alcohol)

OTHER STYLES YOU MAY ENJOY

- English-Style Sweet Stout (Milk Stout)
- Vienna-Style Lager

FRENCH-STYLE BIÈRE DE GARDE

Bière de garde translates as "beer for keeping." Examples of the French-style bière de garde are popping up more and more from US producers. Blond, amber, and brown versions exist. This style is characterized by a toasted malt aroma and slight malt sweetness. Alcohol flavor is evident. Often bottle-conditioned, it can have *Brettanomyces* yeast-derived aromas and flavors that are slightly acidic, fruity, horsey, goaty, and/or leather-like. Earthy, cellar-like, and/or musty aromas are acceptable.

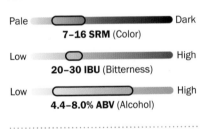

Pale ▬▬▬▬▬▬▬▬ Dark
7–16 SRM (Color)

Low ▬▬▬▬▬▬▬▬ High
20–30 IBU (Bitterness)

Low ▬▬▬▬▬▬▬▬ High
4.4–8.0% ABV (Alcohol)

OTHER STYLES YOU MAY ENJOY

- Vienna-Style Lager
- German-Style Hefeweizen

CATEGORY
HYBRID BEERS

FOOD PAIRINGS

 Roasted lamb with mint

 Soft ripened cheeses

 Pecan pie

GLASSWARE & SERVING TEMPERATURE

 Tulip
45–55°F

INGREDIENTS

Hops: Fuggle

Malt: CaraVienne, Pilsner, Munich, black patent

Yeast: Ale, possibly *Brettanomyces*

CALIFORNIA COMMON

Beers in the California common style are brewed with lager yeast but fermented at ale fermentation temperatures. There is a noticeable degree of toasted malt and/or caramel-like malt character in flavor and often in aroma. Frequently referred to as "steam beer," this style was made famous by San Francisco's Anchor Brewing Company. Hop flavor is low to medium-low and may present as woody, rustic, or minty from the use of Northern Brewer hops.

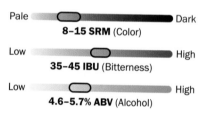

Pale — Dark
8–15 SRM (Color)

Low — High
35–45 IBU (Bitterness)

Low — High
4.6–5.7% ABV (Alcohol)

OTHER STYLES YOU MAY ENJOY

- American Pale Ale
- Vienna-Style Lager
- English-Style IPA

GERMAN-STYLE ALTBIER

Originally from the Düsseldorf area of Germany, German-style *altbier* strikes a balance between flavors and aromas of hops and malt, but can have low levels of fruity esters and some noticeable peppery and floral hop aromas. Before Germany had lager beer, it had ales. *Alt*, meaning "old," pays homage to one rebel region in Germany that did not turn to lagering its beer. Many US brewers celebrate this ale tradition with beautiful examples of this top-fermented German beer style.

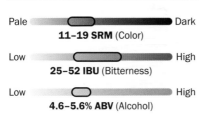

Pale ▬▬▬▬▬▬▬▬▬▬ Dark
11–19 SRM (Color)

Low ▬▬▬▬▬▬▬▬▬▬ High
25–52 IBU (Bitterness)

Low ▬▬▬▬▬▬▬▬▬▬ High
4.6–5.6% ABV (Alcohol)

OTHER STYLES YOU MAY ENJOY

- American Brown Ale
- Belgian-Style Dubbel

CATEGORY
HYBRID BEERS

FOOD PAIRINGS

 Grilled salmon

 Emmental

 Apple pie

GLASSWARE & SERVING TEMPERATURE

 Tulip
45–50°F

INGREDIENTS

Hops: Spalt, Magnum, Tettnang

Malt: Pilsner, Munich, CaraMunich, Carafa Special II, aromatic

Yeast: Ale

GERMAN-STYLE KÖLSCH

Crisp, delicate, and oh-so-drinkable, German-style *Kölsch* has qualities of both lagers and ales. Technically, for beer to be called a Kölsch it must come from the city of Cologne (Köln) in Germany, but that hasn't stopped American craft brewers from embracing Kölsch-style beers. Light in color and malt character, this style's fermentation process yields a light, vinous character, which is accompanied by a slightly dry, crisp finish. A light pear, apple, or Riesling wine-like fruitiness may be apparent.

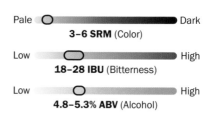

Pale ⬤━━━━━━━ Dark
3–6 SRM (Color)

Low ━⬤━━━━━━ High
18–28 IBU (Bitterness)

Low ━━━⬤━━━━ High
4.8–5.3% ABV (Alcohol)

CATEGORY
HYBRID BEERS

FOOD PAIRINGS

 Bratwurst

 Nutty cheeses

 Light apricot cake

GLASSWARE & SERVING TEMPERATURE

 Flute
40–45°F

INGREDIENTS

Hops: German noble (Hallertau, Spalt, Saaz, Tettnang)

Malt: Pilsner, Vienna

Yeast: Ale

OTHER STYLES YOU MAY ENJOY
- English-Style Pale Ale
- Belgian-Style Witbier

IRISH-STYLE RED ALE

Irish-style red ale is a balanced beer style known for its unique malty taste and lower bitterness and alcohol content. Using a moderate amount of kilned malts and roasted barley in the recipe gives the beer the reddish color for which it is named and a medium, candy-like caramel malt sweetness, and sometimes lends a tan color to the collar of foam on top. This style may contain adjuncts (unmalted ingredients that provide extra fermentable sugars), such as corn, rice, and sugar, which help dry out the beer's finish and lessen the body. With flavor notes of caramel, toffee, and sometimes low-level diacetyl (butter flavor), the Irish red ale beer style also has a modest, approachable hop bitterness.

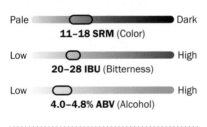

Pale ▬▬▬◖▬▬▬▬ Dark
11–18 SRM (Color)

Low ▬▬◖▬▬▬▬▬ High
20–28 IBU (Bitterness)

Low ▬◖▬▬▬▬▬▬ High
4.0–4.8% ABV (Alcohol)

OTHER STYLES YOU MAY ENJOY

- American Amber Lager
- Belgian-Style Dubbel
- German-Style Weizenbock

FOOD PAIRINGS

 Roasted vegetables

 Cheddar

 Poached pears

GLASSWARE & SERVING TEMPERATURE

Nonic pint
45–55°F

INGREDIENTS

Hops: English varieties (e.g. East Kent Goldings)

Malt: Pale, crystal, roasted barley

Yeast: Lager or ale

PORTER

This long-standing style can be traced back to the English working class of the 1700s, when beer of this style rapidly became popular with street and river porters. A porter is dark in color, with flavors of chocolate, light coffee, nut, and caramel. Porters are less roasty and espresso-like than stouts, but have deeper cocoa flavors than brown ales. Porters are a great beer to have with a wide variety of foods, and a favorite among many craft brewers and their fans.

BEER STYLES

American Imperial Porter

Baltic-Style Porter

English-Style Brown Porter

Robust Porter

Smoke Porter

AMERICAN IMPERIAL PORTER

Definitively American, the imperial porter should have no roasted barley flavors or strong burnt/black malt character. Medium caramel and cocoa-like sweetness is present, with complementing hop character and malt-derived sweetness. Hop aroma and flavor are low to medium-high. Hop bitterness is medium-low to medium. Ale-like fruity ester flavors should be evident but not overpowering.

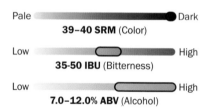

Pale ■■■■■■■■■ Dark
39–40 SRM (Color)

Low ■■■■■■■■■ High
35-50 IBU (Bitterness)

Low ■■■■■■■■■ High
7.0–12.0% ABV (Alcohol)

OTHER STYLES YOU MAY ENJOY

- Chocolate Beer
- German-Style Doppelbock
- Belgian-Style Dubbel

CATEGORY
PORTER

FOOD PAIRINGS

 Chicken mole enchiladas

 Smoked Gouda

 Blondie butterscotch brownies

GLASSWARE & SERVING TEMPERATURE

 Tulip
50–55°F

INGREDIENTS

Hops: Varies

Malt: Varies

Yeast: Ale

BALTIC-STYLE PORTER

Baltic-style porter is a smooth, cold-fermented and cold-lagered beer brewed with lager yeast. Because of its alcoholic strength, it may include very low to low complex alcohol flavors and/or lager fruitiness, such as berries, grapes, and plums (but not banana; ale-like fruitiness from warm-temperature fermentation is not appropriate). This style has the malt flavors of a brown porter and the roast of a schwarzbier but is bigger in alcohol and body. Distinctive malt aromas of caramelized sugars, licorice, and chocolate-like notes of roasted malts and dark sugars are present. Roasted dark malts sometimes contribute a coffee-like roasted barley aroma. A low smoky aroma from malt may be evident. Debittered roasted malts are best used for this style.

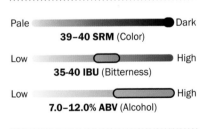

Pale ▬▬▬▬▬▬▬▬▬● Dark
39–40 SRM (Color)

Low ▬▬▬◖▬▬▬▬● High
35-40 IBU (Bitterness)

Low ▬▬▬▬▬◖▬● High
7.0–12.0% ABV (Alcohol)

OTHER STYLES YOU MAY ENJOY

- Robust Porter

- American Imperial Red Ale

- German-Style Doppelbock

ENGLISH-STYLE BROWN PORTER

The English-style brown porter has no roasted barley or strong burnt/black malt character. Low to medium malt sweetness, nutty, bready, caramel, toffee, and chocolate are acceptable. Hop bitterness is medium. Softer, sweeter, and more caramel-like than a robust porter, with less alcohol and body. Fruity esters may be present.

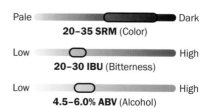

Pale ▬▬▬▬▬▬▬▬▬ Dark
20–35 SRM (Color)

Low ▬▬▬▬▬▬▬▬▬ High
20–30 IBU (Bitterness)

Low ▬▬▬▬▬▬▬▬▬ High
4.5–6.0% ABV (Alcohol)

OTHER STYLES YOU MAY ENJOY
- American-Style Brown Ale
- German-Style Dunkel
- Belgian-Style Dubbel

CATEGORY
PORTER

FOOD PAIRINGS

 Roasted or grilled meats

 Gruyere

 Chocolate peanut butter cookies

GLASSWARE & SERVING TEMPERATURE

 Nonic pint
50–55°F

INGREDIENTS

Hops: English varieties

Malt: British pale ale, brown, crystal, chocolate

Yeast: Ale

ROBUST PORTER

Robust porter features more bitter and roasted malt flavor than brown porter, but not quite as much as stout. Robust porters have a roasted malt flavor, often reminiscent of cocoa, but no roasted barley flavor. They often have grainy, bready, toffee, caramel, chocolate, and coffee characteristics. Their caramel and malty sweetness is in harmony with the sharp bitterness of black malt. Hop bitterness is evident. Diacetyl (butter flavor) is acceptable at very low levels. Fruity esters should be evident, balanced with all other characters.

Porter is the precursor style to stout. With US craft brewers doing so much experimentation with beer styles and ingredients, the lines between certain stouts and porters are often blurred. Yet many distinct examples of the robust porter style do exist.

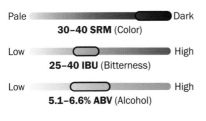

Pale ▬▬▬▬▬▬▬▬▬▬ Dark
30–40 SRM (Color)

Low ▬▬▬▬▬▬▬▬▬▬ High
25–40 IBU (Bitterness)

Low ▬▬▬▬▬▬▬▬▬▬ High
5.1–6.6% ABV (Alcohol)

OTHER STYLES YOU MAY ENJOY
- American Black Ale
- English-Style Sweet Stout (Milk Stout)

CATEGORY
PORTER

FOOD PAIRINGS

 Roasted or grilled meats

 Gruyere

 Chocolate peanut butter cookies

GLASSWARE & SERVING TEMPERATURE

Nonic pint
50–55°F

INGREDIENTS

Hops: English varieties

Malt: Munich, crystal, chocolate, black patent

Yeast: Ale

SMOKE PORTER

Typically, a smoke porter beer is created from a robust porter base that is given smoky depth thanks to wood-smoked malt. Brewers usually cite the specific wood used to smoke the malt, and different woods will lend different flavors to the finished product. Smoke flavors dissipate over time.

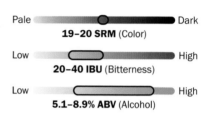

Pale ▬▬▬▬▬⬤▬▬▬▬ Dark
19–20 SRM (Color)

Low ▬▬▬⬤▬▬▬▬▬ High
20–40 IBU (Bitterness)

Low ▬▬▬⬤▬▬▬ High
5.1–8.9% ABV (Alcohol)

OTHER STYLES YOU MAY ENJOY

- English-Style Old Ale
- American Brett
- Herb and Spice Beer

STOUT

Stouts are very dark beers that are fermented at warm temperatures and vary in strength. The name stout comes from the term stout porter, describing a bolder permutation of the porter style so popular during the eighteenth century. Stouts are considered to have stronger roasted flavors than porters, but can vary in character from dry, smooth, and sweet or strong and bitter, depending on the type.

BEER STYLES

American Imperial Stout

American Stout

English-Style Oatmeal Stout

English-Style Sweet Stout (Milk Stout)

Irish-Style Dry Stout

CATEGORY
STOUT

FOOD PAIRINGS

 Foie gras

 Aged cheeses

 Flourless chocolate cake

GLASSWARE & SERVING TEMPERATURE

Snifter
50–55°F

INGREDIENTS

Hops: English varieties

Malt: Pale, black roasted barley, Special "B", CaraMunich, chocolate, pale chocolate

Yeast: Ale

AMERICAN IMPERIAL STOUT

The American imperial stout is the strongest in terms of alcohol and body within the stout family. Black in color, these beers typically have an extremely rich malty flavor and aroma with full, sweet malt character. Bitterness can come from roasted malts or hop additions. Malt flavors can include bittersweet chocolate, cocoa, or coffee. Hop aroma and flavor are medium-high to high, with floral, citrus, and/or herbal hop aromas. Hop bitterness is medium-high to very high and balanced with the malt character.

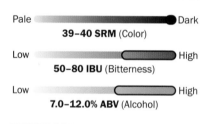

Pale ———————————— Dark
39–40 SRM (Color)

Low ———————————— High
50–80 IBU (Bitterness)

Low ———————————— High
7.0–12.0% ABV (Alcohol)

OTHER STYLES YOU MAY ENJOY
• English-Style Sweet Stout (Milk Stout)

AMERICAN STOUT

Strikingly bold and undeniably beautiful, American stout is a distinct variant of its European counterpart. American stouts blend generous amounts of dark malts exhibiting medium caramel, chocolate, and/or roasted coffee flavor and a distinctive dry-roasted bitterness in the finish. American hop fans will enjoy medium to high hop aroma and flavor, often with American citrus-type and/or resiny hop aromas. The stout is a terrific companion to bold, hearty foods like game meat, but it also pairs particularly well with soups and strong cheeses, in addition to a variety of after-dinner desserts.

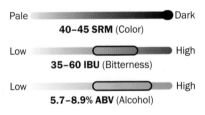

Pale ●──────── Dark
40–45 SRM (Color)

Low ●──────── High
35–60 IBU (Bitterness)

Low ●──────── High
5.7–8.9% ABV (Alcohol)

OTHER STYLES YOU MAY ENJOY

- Irish-Style Dry Stout
- Coffee Beer

CATEGORY
STOUT

FOOD PAIRINGS

 Grilled lamb

 Sharp cheddar

 Coffee cake

GLASSWARE & SERVING TEMPERATURE

Nonic pint
50–55°F

INGREDIENTS

Hops: Horizon, Centennial

Malt: Pale, black roasted barley, chocolate, crystal

Yeast: Ale

ENGLISH-STYLE OATMEAL STOUT

The addition of oatmeal adds a smooth, rich body to the oatmeal stout. The roasted malt character is caramel-like and chocolate-like, and should be smooth and not bitter. Coffee-like roasted barley and malt aromas are prominent. This low- to medium-alcohol style is packed with darker malt flavors and a rich and oily body from oatmeal. Hop aroma and flavor are optional but should not overpower the overall balance if present. Hop bitterness is medium and fruity esters are very low.

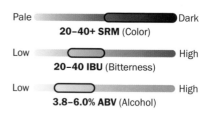

Pale ●━━━━━━━━━━━● Dark
20–40+ SRM (Color)

Low ●━━━━━━━━● High
20–40 IBU (Bitterness)

Low ●━━━━━● High
3.8–6.0% ABV (Alcohol)

OTHER STYLES YOU MAY ENJOY
- Robust Porter

CATEGORY
STOUT

FOOD PAIRINGS

 Chicken in mole sauce

 Aged cheddar

 Sweet potato cheesecake

GLASSWARE & SERVING TEMPERATURE

 Nonic pint
50–55°F

INGREDIENTS

Hops: English varieties

Malt: Pale, flaked oats, chocolate, Victory, crystal, black roasted barley

Yeast: Ale

ENGLISH-STYLE SWEET STOUT (MILK STOUT)

Sweet stout, also referred to as cream stout or milk stout, is black in color. Malt sweetness, chocolate and caramel should dominate the flavor profile and contribute to the aroma. It also should have a low to medium-low roasted malt/barley-derived bitterness. Hop aroma and flavor are not perceived. Hop bitterness is low to medium-low and serves to balance and suppress some of the sweetness without contributing apparent flavor or aroma. Milk sugar (lactose) lends the style more body. This beer does use lactose sugar, so people with lactose intolerance should probably avoid this style.

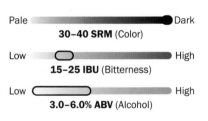

30–40 SRM (Color)
Pale — Dark

15–25 IBU (Bitterness)
Low — High

3.0–6.0% ABV (Alcohol)
Low — High

OTHER STYLES YOU MAY ENJOY

- Barrel-Aged Beer
- American Black Ale

CATEGORY
STOUT

FOOD PAIRINGS

 Mexican mole, spicy BBQ

 Buttery cheddar

 Chocolate cake, ice cream

GLASSWARE & SERVING TEMPERATURE

 Nonic pint
50–55°F

INGREDIENTS

Hops: English varieties

Malt: British pale ale, black patent, pale chocolate, crystal

Yeast: Ale

Initial malt and light caramel flavors give way to a distinctive dry-roasted bitterness in the finish, which is achieved with roasted barley. The emphasis on coffee-like roasted barley and a moderate degree of roasted malt aromas define much of the character. Fruity esters are minimal and overshadowed by malt, high hop bitterness, and roasted barley character. Hop bitterness is medium to medium high, while hop aroma and flavor are not perceived to low, from English-type hops. This beer is often dispensed via nitrogen gas taps that lend a smooth, creamy body to the mouthfeel.

CATEGORY
STOUT

FOOD PAIRINGS

 Seafood (oysters), ham

 Irish cheddar

 Chocolate desserts

GLASSWARE & SERVING TEMPERATURE

 Nonic pint
50–55°F

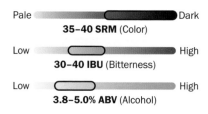

Pale	Dark
35–40 SRM (Color)	

Low	High
30–40 IBU (Bitterness)	

Low	High
3.8–5.0% ABV (Alcohol)	

INGREDIENTS

Hops: English varieties

Malt: British pale ale, flaked barley, black roasted barley

Yeast: Ale

OTHER STYLES YOU MAY ENJOY

- English-Style Brown Ale
- German-Style Schwarzbier
- Belgian-Style Dubbel

BOCK

Bock beers are stronger bottom-fermented, lager-style beers. Robustly malty, the flavors of bock round out during lagering. This malt-forward family of beers is quite versatile and pairs with all types of food.

BEER STYLES

German-Style Bock

German-Style Doppelbock

German-Style Maibock

German-Style Weizenbock

GERMAN-STYLE BOCK

Traditional bock beers are all-malt brews and are high in malt sweetness. Malt character should be a balance of sweetness and toasted or nut-like malt. Hop flavor is low and bitterness is perceived as medium, increasing proportionately with starting gravity. Fruity-ester aromas should be minimal, if present. The German word *bock* translates as "goat"!

CATEGORY
BOCK

FOOD PAIRINGS

 Grilled rib eye

 Aged Swiss

 Chocolate

GLASSWARE & SERVING TEMPERATURE

 Tulip
45–50°F

INGREDIENTS

Hops: German noble (Hallertau, Spalt, Saaz, Tettnang)

Malt: Pilsner, Munich, CaraMunich, Melanoidin

Yeast: Lager

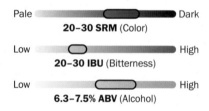

Pale ——————— Dark
20–30 SRM (Color)

Low ——————— High
20–30 IBU (Bitterness)

Low ——————— High
6.3–7.5% ABV (Alcohol)

OTHER STYLES YOU MAY ENJOY

- Belgian-Style Dubbel
- American Amber Lager

GERMAN-STYLE DOPPELBOCK

Doppel meaning "double," this style is a bigger and stronger version of the lower-gravity German-style bock. Made by monks in Munich, *doppelbock* was historically brewed and consumed by monks fasting during Lent. The doppelbock style is very food-friendly, the beers being rich in melanoidins reminiscent of toasted bread. Malty sweetness is dominant but should not be cloying. Malt character is more reminiscent of fresh and lightly toasted Munich-style malt, more so than caramel or toffee malt. Doppelbocks are full-bodied, and alcoholic strength is on the higher end. Some examples may have prune, plum, or grape esters.

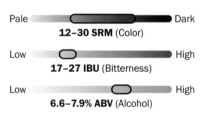

Pale ▬▬▬▬▬ Dark
12–30 SRM (Color)

Low ▬▬▬▬▬ High
17–27 IBU (Bitterness)

Low ▬▬▬▬▬ High
6.6–7.9% ABV (Alcohol)

OTHER STYLES YOU MAY ENJOY

- Scotch Ale/Wee Heavy
- English-Style Old Ale

CATEGORY
BOCK

FOOD PAIRINGS

 Pork or ham

 Strong cheeses

 German chocolate cake

GLASSWARE & SERVING TEMPERATURE

Tulip
45–50°F

INGREDIENTS

Hops: German noble (Hallertau, Spalt, Saaz, Tettnang)

Malt: Pilsner, Munich, Vienna, CaraMunich

Yeast: Lager

GERMAN-STYLE MAIBOCK

Also called *helles* bock (meaning "pale bock"), German-style *maibock* is paler in color and more hop-centric than traditional bock beers. A lightly toasted and/or bready malt character is often evident. Roasted or heavy toast/caramel malt aromas should be absent. Hop aroma and flavor are low to medium-low, deriving from noble-type hops. Fruity-ester flavors may be low, if present. Hop bitterness is also low.

CATEGORY
BOCK

FOOD PAIRINGS

 Ham

 Swiss

 White chocolate cheesecake

GLASSWARE & SERVING TEMPERATURE

 Goblet
45–55°F

INGREDIENTS

Hops: German noble (Hallertau, Spalt, Saaz, Tettnang)

Malt: Pilsner, Munich, Vienna

Yeast: Lager

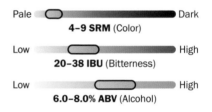

Pale ⬭══════════ Dark
4–9 SRM (Color)

Low ═══⬭══════ High
20–38 IBU (Bitterness)

Low ══════⬭═══ High
6.0–8.0% ABV (Alcohol)

OTHER STYLES YOU MAY ENJOY

- Belgian-Style Golden Strong Ale
- American Brown Ale

GERMAN-STYLE WEIZENBOCK

The German-style *weizenbock* is a wheat version of German-style bock, or a bigger and beefier dunkelweizen. Malt melanoidins and weizen ale yeast are the star ingredients. If served with yeast the appearance may be very cloudy, which is appropriate for the style. Medium malty sweetness is present. If dark, a mild roasted malt aroma and flavor should emerge, with flavors of bready malt and dark fruits like plum, raisin, and grape. This style is low on bitterness and high on carbonation. Yeast-derived, balanced clove-like phenols and fruity, banana-like esters produce a well-rounded aroma.

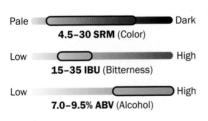

Pale ▬▬▬▬▬ Dark
4.5–30 SRM (Color)

Low ▬▬▬▬▬ High
15–35 IBU (Bitterness)

Low ▬▬▬▬▬ High
7.0–9.5% ABV (Alcohol)

OTHER STYLES YOU MAY ENJOY

- American-Style Wheat Wine Ale
- Belgian-Style Tripel
- Fruit and Field Beer

SCOTTISH-STYLE ALE

Scottish ales are overwhelmingly malty, with a rich and dominant sweet malt flavor and aroma. A caramel character is often part of the profile. Some examples feature a light smoked peat flavor.

BEER STYLES

Scottish-Style Ale

Scotch Ale/Wee Heavy

SCOTTISH-STYLE ALE

Scottish-style ales vary depending on strength and flavor, but in general retain a malt-forward character with some degree of caramel-like or toffee malt flavors and a soft and chewy mouthfeel. Hops do not play a huge role in this style. The numbers commonly associated with brands of this style (e.g., 60/, 70/, 80/, and so on) originate with the Scottish tradition of listing the cost, in shillings, of a hogshead (large cask) of beer, with the price reflecting the relative strength of the beer.

CATEGORY
SCOTTISH-STYLE ALE

FOOD PAIRINGS

 Variety of meats, including game

 Pungent cheeses

 Creamy desserts with fruit

GLASSWARE & SERVING TEMPERATURE

 Thistle
50–55°F

INGREDIENTS

Hops: English varieties

Malt: Pale malt, crystal malt, and chocolate malt

Yeast: Ale

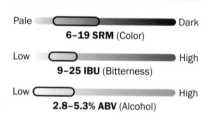

Pale		Dark

6–19 SRM (Color)

Low		High

9–25 IBU (Bitterness)

Low		High

2.8–5.3% ABV (Alcohol)

OTHER STYLES YOU MAY ENJOY

- English-Style Brown Ale
- Belgian-Style Dubbel
- Barrel-Aged Beer

SCOTCH ALE/WEE HEAVY

Scotch ale, or wee heavy, is overwhelmingly malty, with a rich and dominant sweet malt flavor and aroma. A caramel character is often part of the profile. Some examples feature a light smoked peat flavor. This style could be considered the Scottish version of an English-style barleywine. Overly smoked versions would be considered specialty examples.

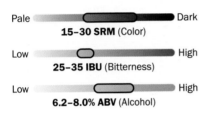

Pale ▬▬▬▬▬▬▬▬ Dark
15–30 SRM (Color)

Low ▬▬▬▬▬▬▬▬ High
25–35 IBU (Bitterness)

Low ▬▬▬▬▬▬▬▬ High
6.2–8.0% ABV (Alcohol)

OTHER STYLES YOU MAY ENJOY
- German-Style Doppelbock

WILD/SOUR BEERS

Wild and sour beers are produced through any combination of conventional brewing yeast in addition to the introduction of unconventional brewing yeast, like *Brettanomyces*, or acidifying bacteria, such as *Lactobacillus* or *Pediococcus*. These unconventional "wild" microorganisms are intentionally used to add complexity.

BEER STYLES

American Brett

American Sour

Belgian-Style Flanders

Belgian-Style Fruit Lambic

Belgian-Style Lambic/Gueuze

Contemporary Gose

AMERICAN BRETT

These unique beers vary in color and can take on the hues of added fruits or other ingredients. Horsey, goaty, leathery, phenolic, and some fruity acidic character derived from *Brettanomyces* may be evident, but these should be in balance with the other components of the beer. Despite how *Brettanomyces* presents in sour beer, American Brett beers do not exhibit the level of sour taste that sour beers do, thus, Brett beers should not be mistaken for a sour beer.

CATEGORY
WILD/SOUR BEERS

FOOD PAIRINGS

 Grilled or roasted game

 Earthy farmhouse cheeses

 Fruit-filled pastries

Pale ◖━━━━━━━━━◗ Dark
SRM Varies (Color)

Low ◖━━━━━━━━━◗ High
IBU Varies (Bitterness)

Low ◖━━━━━━━━━◗ High
ABV Varies (Alcohol)

GLASSWARE & SERVING TEMPERATURE

 Tulip
45–55°F

OTHER STYLES YOU MAY ENJOY
- Belgian-Style Tripel
- German-Style Pilsner

INGREDIENTS

Hops: Varies

Malt: Varies

Yeast: *Brettanomyces*, ale/lager possible

AMERICAN SOUR

The acidity present in American sour beer is usually in the form of lactic, acetic, and other organic acids naturally developed with acidified malt in the mash or produced during fermentation using various microorganisms. These beers may derive their sour flavor from pure cultured forms of souring agents or from the influence of barrel aging. Hop aroma, flavor, and bitterness are evident over the full range from low to high.

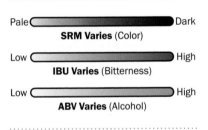

Pale ▭ Dark
SRM Varies (Color)

Low ▭ High
IBU Varies (Bitterness)

Low ▭ High
ABV Varies (Alcohol)

OTHER STYLES YOU MAY ENJOY

- Belgian-Style Witbier

- American Wheat

- Barrel-Aged Beer

BELGIAN-STYLE FLANDERS

Belgian-style Flanders is an ale style with character and balance, thanks to lactic sourness and acetic acid. Cherry-like flavors are acceptable, as is malt sweetness that can lend a cocoa-like character. Oak or other wood-like flavors may be present, even if the beer was not aged in barrels. Overall, the style is characterized by slight to strong lactic sourness, and Flanders "reds" sometimes include a balanced degree of acetic acid. *Brettanomyces*-derived flavors may be absent or very low. This style is a marvel in flavor complexity, combining malt, yeast, microorganisms, acidity, and low astringency from a process of barrel aging.

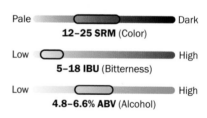

Pale ⬛ Dark
12–25 SRM (Color)

Low ⬛ High
5–18 IBU (Bitterness)

Low ⬛ High
4.8–6.6% ABV (Alcohol)

OTHER STYLES YOU MAY ENJOY

- American Brown Ale
- Vienna-Style Lager
- Fruit and Field Beer

BELGIAN-STYLE FRUIT LAMBIC

Often known as *cassis, framboise, kriek,* or *pêche*, a fruit *lambic* takes on the color and flavor of the fruit it is brewed with. Fruit lambic can be dry or sweet, clear or cloudy—it all depends on the ingredients. Notes of *Brettanomyces* are often present at varied levels. Sourness is an important part of the flavor profile, though sweetness may compromise the intensity. These flavored lambics may be very dry or mildly sweet.

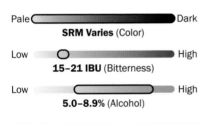

Pale ▢ Dark
SRM Varies (Color)

Low ◯ High
15–21 IBU (Bitterness)

Low ▢ High
5.0–8.9% (Alcohol)

OTHER STYLES YOU MAY ENJOY
- Honey Beer
- American Sour

BELGIAN-STYLE LAMBIC/GUEUZE

Belgian-style lambic or *gueuze* beers are naturally and spontaneously fermented with high to very high levels of esters, plus bacterial and yeast-derived sourness that sometimes includes acetic flavors. Lambic-style beers are not blended, whereas the gueuze style involves blending old and new lambic-style beers, the blend then being re-fermented in the bottle. Historically, lambics and gueuze are dry and completely attenuated, exhibiting no residual sweetness either from malt, sugar, or artificial sweeteners. Characteristic horsey, goaty, leathery, and phenolic aromas derived from *Brettanomyces* yeast are often present at moderate levels.

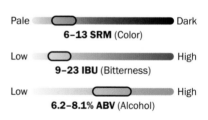

Pale ▢ Dark
6–13 SRM (Color)

Low ▢ High
9–23 IBU (Bitterness)

Low ▢ High
6.2–8.1% ABV (Alcohol)

OTHER STYLES YOU MAY ENJOY

- Fruit and Field Beer
- German-Style Hefeweizen
- American Sour

CONTEMPORARY GOSE

Straw to medium amber, the contemporary Gose is cloudy from suspended yeast. A wide variety of herbal, spice, floral, or fruity aromas are present, in harmony with other aromas. These various additional aromas are not found in traditional Leipzig-style Gose. Salt (table salt) character is traditional in low amounts, but may vary from absent to present. Body is low to medium-low. Low to medium lactic acid character is evident in all examples as a sharp, refreshing sourness.

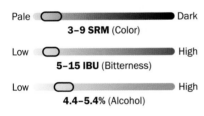

Pale ⬤━━━━━━━ Dark
3–9 SRM (Color)

Low ⬤━━━━━━━ High
5–15 IBU (Bitterness)

Low ━⬤━━━━━━ High
4.4–5.4% (Alcohol)

OTHER STYLES YOU MAY ENJOY

- Berliner-Style Weisse

- Session Beer

PILSNER AND PALE LAGER

The original hoppy, pale beer style, Pilsners offer clean, bready maltiness and plenty of hop character. Classic interpretations can be traced back to areas of Germany and what is now the Czech Republic. When exploring this style, take note of the fuller-bodied Bohemian styles, reminiscent of Czech versions, compared to the thinner German-style interpretations—these characteristics are mostly attributed to the water character of each region.

BEER STYLES

American Lager

German-Style Helles

Bohemian-Style Pilsner

German-Style Pilsner

European-Style Export

AMERICAN LAGER

American lager has little in the way of hop and malt character. This beer style is straw to gold in color, is very clean, crisp, and highly carbonated.

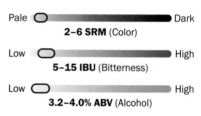

Pale ⬤━━━━━━━━ Dark
2–6 SRM (Color)

Low ⬤━━━━━━━━ High
5–15 IBU (Bitterness)

Low ⬤━━━━━━━━ High
3.2–4.0% ABV (Alcohol)

OTHER STYLES YOU MAY ENJOY

- German-Style Schwarzbier
- Session Beer
- European-Style Export

BOHEMIAN-STYLE PILSNER

The Bohemian Pilsner has a slightly sweet and evident malt character that is toasted, biscuit-like, and bready. Hop bitterness is perceived as medium with a low to medium-low level of noble-type hop aroma and flavor. This style originated in 1842, with *Pilsner* originally indicating an appellation in the Czech Republic. Classic examples of this style used to be conditioned in wooden tanks and had a less sharp hop bitterness despite the IBU range being similar to German-style Pilsner. Low-level diacetyl (buttery flavor) is acceptable. Bohemian-style Pilsners are darker in color and higher in final gravity than their German counterparts.

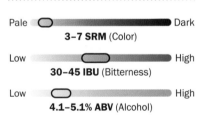

Pale ○━━━━━━━━━━ Dark
3–7 SRM (Color)

Low ━━━━━○━━━━━ High
30–45 IBU (Bitterness)

Low ━━○━━━━━━━━ High
4.1–5.1% ABV (Alcohol)

OTHER STYLES YOU MAY ENJOY
- English-Style IPA
- American Wheat
- German-Style Kölsch

CATEGORY
PILSNER & PALE LAGER

FOOD PAIRINGS

 Shellfish, chicken, salads

 Mild white cheddar

 Shortbread cookies

GLASSWARE & SERVING TEMPERATURE

 Flute
40–45°F

INGREDIENTS

Hops: Czech Saaz

Malt: Pilsner, Carapils®

Yeast: Lager

EUROPEAN-STYLE EXPORT

Sometimes referred to as a Dortmunder export, the European-style export has the malt-forward flavor and sweetness of a German-style *helles*, but the bitter base of a German-style Pilsner. This lager is all about balance, with medium hop character and firm but low malt sweetness. Look for toasted malt flavors and spicy floral hop aromas.

CATEGORY
PILSNER & PALE LAGER

FOOD PAIRINGS

 Grilled steak

 Chèvre

 Bread pudding

GLASSWARE & SERVING TEMPERATURE

 Flute
40–45°F

INGREDIENTS

Hops: German noble (Hallertau, Spalt, Saaz, Tettnang)

Malt: Pilsner, Munich

Yeast: Lager

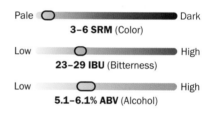

Pale ⬤━━━━━ Dark
3–6 SRM (Color)

Low ━━⬤━━━━ High
23–29 IBU (Bitterness)

Low ━━⬤━━━━ High
5.1–6.1% ABV (Alcohol)

OTHER STYLES YOU MAY ENJOY
- Blonde Ale
- Belgian-Style Saison
- American Wheat

GERMAN-STYLE HELLES

Helles means "pale in color," as these beers are often golden. The German-style helles lager is a bit rounder, or fuller-bodied, than light lager and even all-malt Pilsner. Helles lager offers a touch of sweetness that balances a measurable addition of spicy German hop flavor and light bitterness. The malt character is soft and bready, making it a terrific complement to light dishes, such as salads, or fresh shellfish, like clams. Clean and crisp, this is a refreshing beer with substance. Low levels of yeast-derived sulfur aromas and flavors may be common.

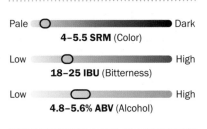

Pale	Dark
4–5.5 SRM (Color)	

Low	High
18–25 IBU (Bitterness)	

Low	High
4.8–5.6% ABV (Alcohol)	

OTHER STYLES YOU MAY ENJOY
- Blonde Ale
- German-Style Kölsch

CATEGORY
PILSNER & PALE LAGER

FOOD PAIRINGS

 Samosas

 Colby

 Baklava

GLASSWARE & SERVING TEMPERATURE

 Flute
45–50°F

INGREDIENTS

Hops: German noble (Hallertau, Spalt, Saaz, Tettnang)

Malt: Pilsner, Munich

Yeast: Lager

GERMAN-STYLE PILSNER

Some of the first breweries in the United States were started in the 1800s by German immigrants and specialized in brewing Pilsners. Since then, American craft brewers have continued to experiment with the classic "pils" style. Like other German beers, Pilsner lager's crisp finish makes for a refreshing beer during the warmer months of the year.

Classic German-style Pilsners have a malty sweetness that can be perceived in aroma and flavor. Distinctly different from the Bohemian-style Pilsner, this style is lighter in color and body, and the noble-type hop aroma and flavor are moderate and more obvious.

CATEGORY
PILSNER & PALE LAGER

FOOD PAIRINGS

 Shellfish, chicken, salads

 White cheddar

 Shortbread cookies

GLASSWARE & SERVING TEMPERATURE

 Flute
40–45°F

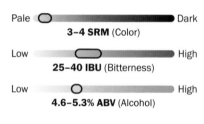

Pale ⬤━━━━━━━━ Dark
3–4 SRM (Color)

Low ━━━⬤━━━━ High
25–40 IBU (Bitterness)

Low ━━⬤━━━━━ High
4.6–5.3% ABV (Alcohol)

INGREDIENTS

Hops: German noble (Hallertau, Spalt, Saaz, Tettnang)

Malt: Pilsner, Munich

Yeast: Lager

OTHER STYLES YOU MAY ENJOY
- American Pale Ale
- Belgian-Style Tripel
- English-Style IPA

SPECIALTY BEER

This style is a catch-all for any type of beer—ale, lager, or otherwise—that does not fit neatly into another contemporary style family. These beers are often based on classic styles, but with added experimental twists. No ingredient or process should be discounted, but, generally speaking, the root style can still be recognized. Note that, because these specialty beers can follow any style, some of the specifics for color, bitterness, alcohol, malts, and hops have not been included because there are no quantifiable ranges.

BEER STYLES

American Black Ale	Gluten-Free Beer	Session Beer
Barrel-Aged Beer	Herb and Spice Beer	Smoke Beer
Chocolate Beer	Honey Beer	Specialty Beer
Coffee Beer	Pumpkin Beer	
Fruit and Field Beers	Rye Beer	

AMERICAN BLACK ALE

American black ale is characterized by the perception of caramel malt and dark roasted malt flavor and aroma. Hop bitterness is perceived to be medium-high to high. Hop flavor and aroma are medium-high. Fruity, citrus, piney, floral, and herbal character from hops of all origins may contribute to the overall experience. This beer is often called black IPA or Cascadian dark ale.

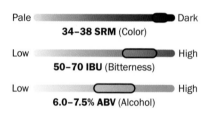

Pale ⬤ Dark
34–38 SRM (Color)

Low ⬤ High
50–70 IBU (Bitterness)

Low ⬤ High
6.0–7.5% ABV (Alcohol)

OTHER STYLES YOU MAY ENJOY

- Robust Porter
- American Sour
- American IPA

BARREL-AGED BEER

A wood- or barrel-aged beer is any lager, ale, or hybrid beer, either a traditional style or a unique experimental beer, that has been aged for a period of time in a wooden barrel or in contact with wood. The beer is aged with the intention of imparting the unique character of the wood and/or the flavor of what had previously been in the barrel. Beer may be aged in wooden barrels (new or previously used to age wine or spirits), or chips, spirals, and cubes may be added to the conditioning tanks that are normally used to store beer. A variety of types of wood are used including, among others, oak, apple, alder, and hickory. The interior of most barrels is charred or toasted to further enhance the flavor of the wood.

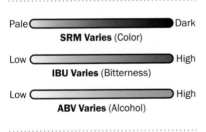

Pale ⊂⬛⬛⬛⬛⬛⬛⬛⬛⬛⟩ Dark
SRM Varies (Color)

Low ⊂⬛⬛⬛⬛⬛⬛⬛⬛⟩ High
IBU Varies (Bitterness)

Low ⊂⬛⬛⬛⬛⟩ High
ABV Varies (Alcohol)

OTHER STYLES YOU MAY ENJOY

- American Brett
- American Sour

CATEGORY
SPECIALTY BEER

FOOD PAIRINGS

 Varies

Varies

 Varies

GLASSWARE & SERVING TEMPERATURE

 Tulip
50–55°F

INGREDIENTS

Hops: Varies

Malt: Varies

Yeast: Lager or ale, may have *Brettanomyces* character

CHOCOLATE BEER

Traditionally added to porters, stouts, and brown ales, where the malt ingredients better complement it, chocolate or cocoa can be added to other styles as well. Chocolate character can range from subtle to overt, but any chocolate beer is generally expected to offer some balance between beer and bonbon. The style can vary greatly in approach as well as flavor profile depending on the brewer.

Chocolate-flavored beer may seem like an odd concept, but any beer or chocolate lover owes it to themselves to give chocolate beer a try.

CATEGORY
SPECIALTY BEER

FOOD PAIRINGS

 Venison mole

 Aged goat cheeses

 Raspberry torte

GLASSWARE & SERVING TEMPERATURE

 Snifter
50–55°F

INGREDIENTS

Hops: Varies

Malt: Varies

Yeast: Lager or Ale

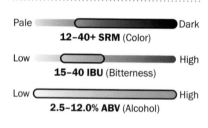

Pale ▬▬▬▬▬▬▬▬▬▬ Dark
12–40+ SRM (Color)

Low ▬▬▬▬▬▬▬▬▬▬ High
15–40 IBU (Bitterness)

Low ▬▬▬▬▬▬▬▬▬▬ High
2.5–12.0% ABV (Alcohol)

OTHER STYLES YOU MAY ENJOY

- Coffee Beer
- English-Style Sweet Stout (Milk Stout)
- American Imperial Porter

COFFEE BEER

If you had to combine two beverages that Americans love, you would have coffee beer. Coffee is a versatile ingredient in beer and lends a smooth roasted flavor to just about any style, from stouts and porters to pale ales and even sour beers. Brewers may steep the beans in either water or beer to impart java flavor while taking care to avoid the addition of too much acidity. Pairing coffee beers with desserts might be an obvious choice, but there is no reason a coffee beer cannot be an excellent companion to a charcoal-grilled rib eye steak at your next cookout. This beer style also makes a nice partner when paired with aged semi-hard cheeses when you're entertaining.

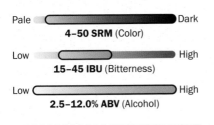

Pale ▬▬▬▬▬▬ Dark
4–50 SRM (Color)

Low ▬▬▬▬▬▬ High
15–45 IBU (Bitterness)

Low ▬▬▬▬▬▬ High
2.5–12.0% ABV (Alcohol)

OTHER STYLES YOU MAY ENJOY

- Irish-Style Dry Stout
- English-Style Sweet Stout (Milk Stout)
- Chocolate Beer

CATEGORY
SPECIALTY BEER

FOOD PAIRINGS

 Pork tenderloin

 Aged semi-hard cheeses

 Vanilla ice cream

GLASSWARE & SERVING TEMPERATURE

 Nonic pint
50–55°F

INGREDIENTS

Hops: Varies

Malt: Varies

Yeast: Lager or ale

FRUIT AND FIELD BEERS

Fruit beer is made with fruit, or fruit extracts that are added during any portion of the brewing process, providing obvious yet harmonious fruit qualities. This idea is expanded to field beers, which use vegetables and herbs in similar fashion.

FOOD PAIRINGS

 Salads

 Creamy cheeses

 Vanilla ice cream

GLASSWARE & SERVING TEMPERATURE

 Tulip
50–55°F

INGREDIENTS

Hops: Varies

Malt: Varies

Yeast: Lager or ale

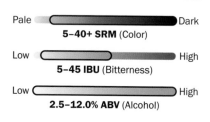

Pale		Dark
5–40+ SRM (Color)		

Low		High
5–45 IBU (Bitterness)		

Low		High
2.5–12.0% ABV (Alcohol)		

OTHER STYLES YOU MAY ENJOY

- Belgian-Style Lambic/Gueuze
- Barrel-Aged Beer
- American Sour

GLUTEN-FREE BEER

If you are one of the two million Americans who suffer from celiac disease, trying craft beer may seem impossible, or at least challenging. Many craft breweries who make gluten-free beers have turned to malted sorghum and buckwheat, which are grains that do not contain gluten, to brew beers for their gluten-averse customers. Dedicated gluten-free breweries have also found success catering to people dealing with gluten intolerance, as well as health-minded beer drinkers who choose to follow a gluten-reduced or gluten-free diet but don't want to give up their favorite beverage.

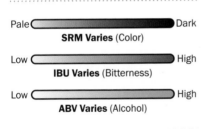

Pale ▢▢▢▢▢▢▢▢▢▢ Dark
SRM Varies (Color)

Low ▢▢▢▢▢▢▢▢▢▢ High
IBU Varies (Bitterness)

Low ▢▢▢▢▢▢▢▢▢▢ High
ABV Varies (Alcohol)

CATEGORY
SPECIALTY BEER

FOOD PAIRINGS

 Varies

 Varies

 Varies

GLASSWARE & SERVING TEMPERATURE

Flute
50–55°F

INGREDIENTS

Hops: Varies

Malt: Varies

Yeast: Lager or ale

HERB AND SPICE BEER

An herb and spice beer is a lager or ale that contains flavors derived from flowers, roots, or seeds. Typically, the hop character is low, allowing the added ingredient to shine through. The appearance, mouthfeel, and aromas vary depending on the herb or spice used. This beer style encompasses innovative examples as well as traditional holiday and winter ales.

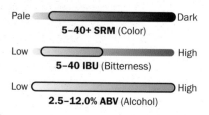

Pale ⟨───────────⟩ Dark
5–40+ SRM (Color)

Low ⟨───────────⟩ High
5–40 IBU (Bitterness)

Low ⟨───────────⟩ High
2.5–12.0% ABV (Alcohol)

OTHER STYLES YOU MAY ENJOY

- Belgian-Style Witbier

- Honey Beer

HONEY BEER

Both lagers and ales can be brewed with honey. Some brewers will choose to experiment with ingredients, while others will add honey to traditional styles. Overall, the character of honey should be evident but not totally overwhelming. A wide variety of honey beers are available. American brewers may add honey to the boil kettle (as a sugar source) or post-boil (to preserve more volatile aromatics).

Pale 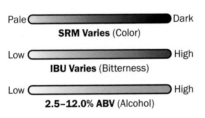 Dark
SRM Varies (Color)

Low High
IBU Varies (Bitterness)

Low High
2.5–12.0% ABV (Alcohol)

OTHER STYLES YOU MAY ENJOY

- Blonde Ale
- German-Style Helles
- Herb and Spice Beer

CATEGORY
SPECIALTY BEER

FOOD PAIRINGS

 Bruschetta

 Ricotta

 Lemon basil gelato

GLASSWARE & SERVING TEMPERATURE

 Tulip
50–55°F

INGREDIENTS

Hops: Varies

Malt: Varies

Yeast: Lager or ale

PUMPKIN BEER

Perhaps the most seasonal of seasonal beers, the pumpkin beer style can be brewed with pumpkin, just pumpkin spices, or even winter squash. Since the fruit does not have much of a taste by itself, many craft brewers have taken to adding spices typically found in pumpkin pie, like cinnamon and clove. However, these flavors should not overpower the beer. Pumpkin can be found in everything from stouts to pale ales and Pilsners. Pumpkin-flavored beers can range from relatively light to dark, bitter to malt forward, and sessionable to high-alcohol.

CATEGORY
SPECIALTY BEER

FOOD PAIRINGS

 Roasted turkey

 Camembert

 Coffee ice cream

GLASSWARE & SERVING TEMPERATURE

 Tulip
50–55°F

INGREDIENTS

Hops: Varies

Malt: Varies

Yeast: Lager or ale

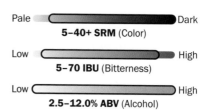

Pale ▬▬▬▬▬▬ Dark
5–40+ SRM (Color)

Low ▬▬▬▬▬▬ High
5–70 IBU (Bitterness)

Low ▬▬▬▬▬▬ High
2.5–12.0% ABV (Alcohol)

OTHER STYLES YOU MAY ENJOY

- Chocolate Beer
- American Brown Ale
- Herb and Spice Beer

RYE BEER

The addition of rye to a beer can add a spicy or pumpernickel character to the flavor and finish. Color is also enhanced by the use of rye and so the beer may become redder. Rye has come into vogue in recent years as an ingredient in everything from stouts to lagers, but it is especially popular with craft brewers in IPAs. To be considered an example of the style, the malt ingredients—the grain bill—should include enough rye so that rye character is evident in the beer. In darker versions, malt flavor can optionally include a low level of roasted malt character (evident as cocoa/chocolate or caramel) and/or aromatic toffee-like, caramel, or biscuit-like characters. A low level of roasted malt astringency is acceptable when balanced with low to medium malt sweetness.

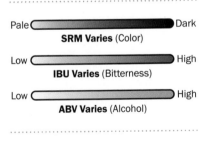

Pale ⬤━━━━━━━━━━⬤ Dark
SRM Varies (Color)

Low ⬤━━━━━━━━━━⬤ High
IBU Varies (Bitterness)

Low ⬤━━━━━━━━━━⬤ High
ABV Varies (Alcohol)

OTHER STYLES YOU MAY ENJOY

- Herb and Spice Beer
- Coffee Beer

CATEGORY
SPECIALTY BEER

FOOD PAIRINGS

 Jerk chicken

 Wensleydale

 Savory bread pudding

GLASSWARE & SERVING TEMPERATURE

 Vase
45–55°F

INGREDIENTS

Hops: Varies

Malt: Varies

Yeast: Lager or ale

CATEGORY
SPECIALTY BEER

FOOD PAIRINGS

 Varies

 Varies

 Varies

GLASSWARE & SERVING TEMPERATURE

 Varies based on style

INGREDIENTS

Hops: Varies

Malt: Varies

Yeast: Lager or ale

SESSION BEER

A session beer is not defined by its flavors or aromas, which can place it in almost any style category. Instead, what makes a session beer is primarily refreshment and drinkability. Any style of beer can be made lower in strength than that described in the conventional style guidelines. The goal should be to reach a balance between the style's character and the lower alcohol content. Drinkability is a factor in the overall balance of these beers. A session beer should not exceed five percent alcohol by volume.

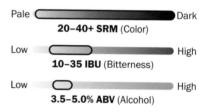

Pale ⬤━━━━━━━━━ Dark
20–40+ SRM (Color)

Low ━━⬤━━━━━ High
10–35 IBU (Bitterness)

Low ━⬤━━━━━━ High
3.5–5.0% ABV (Alcohol)

OTHER STYLES YOU MAY ENJOY
- Irish-Style Dry Stout
- German-Style Kölsch

SMOKE BEER

When malt is kilned over an open flame the smoke flavor becomes infused into the beer, leaving a taste that can vary from dense campfire to slight wisps of smoke. Any style of beer can be smoked; the goal is to reach a balance between the style's character and the smoky properties. Originating in Germany as *rauchbier*, this style is open to interpretation by US craft brewers. Classic base styles include German-style Märzen/Oktoberfest, German-style bock, German-style dunkel, Vienna-style lager, and more. Smoke flavors dissipate over time.

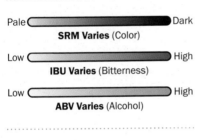

Pale ⊂━━━━━━━⊃ Dark
SRM Varies (Color)

Low ⊂━━━━━━━⊃ High
IBU Varies (Bitterness)

Low ⊂━━━━━━━⊃ High
ABV Varies (Alcohol)

OTHER STYLES YOU MAY ENJOY

- English-Style Old Ale
- American Brett
- Herb and Spice Beer

CATEGORY
SPECIALTY BEER

FOOD PAIRINGS

 Grilled vegetables

 Parmesan

 Gingerbread cookies

GLASSWARE & SERVING TEMPERATURE

 Nonic pint
45–55°F

INGREDIENTS

Hops: Varies

Malt: Varies

Yeast: Lager or ale

FOOD PAIRINGS

 Varies

 Varies

 Varies

GLASSWARE & SERVING
TEMPERATURE

 Snifter
45–55°F

INGREDIENTS

Hops: Varies

Malt: Varies

Yeast: Lager or ale

SPECIALTY BEER

Ingredients used in a specialty beer should be distinctive and evident in either the aroma, flavor, or overall balance of the beer. This style category is a catch-all. Any specialty beer that does not fit other specialty beer styles would be appropriately considered here. Examples can include *sahti*, *roggenbier*, and *steinbier*.

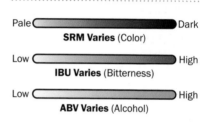

Pale — Dark
SRM Varies (Color)

Low — High
IBU Varies (Bitterness)

Low — High
ABV Varies (Alcohol)

OTHER STYLES YOU MAY ENJOY

- Belgian-Style Fruit Lambic
- Herb and Spice Beer
- American Brett

PAIRING FOOD AND CRAFT BEER

For years, beer was relegated to the most common of foods, but craft brewers are raising the bar. Along with bringing flavor to beer, American craft brewers have opened up a whole new world in food and beer pairing. *Of course* beer goes with pizza, burgers, wings, and chili! But with the myriad flavors available in beer, it's time to experiment. Malty beers can add richness to a dish, while bright, fresh, hoppy offerings can cleanse a palate to make you want to take another bite. Experiment using this guide and then branch out to try new things on your own.

BEER AND FOOD PAIRING GUIDE

The CraftBeer.com Beer and Food Pairing Guide approaches pairing by first looking at common individual food components and comparing them to the six main beer flavor categories: **crisp and clean**; **malty and sweet**; **dark and roasty**; **hoppy and bitter**; **fruity and spicy**; and **sour, tart and funky**. The potential interactions between the food and beer are outlined and an approachable dish is recommended.

FOOD COMPONENT
GRAIN

EXAMPLES

- Farro
- Arborio
- Wild rice
- Polenta

BEER FLAVORS
CRISP & CLEAN

EXAMPLES

 American Amber Lager

 Bohemian-Style Pilsner

INTERACTIONS

Complementary grain flavors
balance hops while remaining
light on the palate.

Example Dish: Creamy risotto

FOOD COMPONENT
BEANS & LEGUMES

BEER FLAVORS
MALTY & SWEET

EXAMPLES

- Lentils
- Fava
- Chickpea
- Green beans

EXAMPLES

  English-Style Brown Ale

  German-Style Hefeweizen

INTERACTIONS

Food adds richness to the beer
while balancing salt and acidity.

Example Dish: Grilled halibut with pole beans

FOOD COMPONENT
SHELLFISH

EXAMPLES

- Clams
- Scallops
- Lobster
- Crab

BEER FLAVORS
FRUITY & SPICY

EXAMPLES

Belgian-Style Saison

German-Style Hefeweizen

INTERACTIONS

Beer brings out salinity and
natural sweetness while
cleansing the palate.

Example Dish: Mussels with garlic, parsley, and butter

FOOD COMPONENT
RICH MEATS & ROOT VEGETABLES

BEER FLAVORS
SOUR, TART & FUNKY

EXAMPLES

- Parsnips
- Carrots
- Beef strip loin
- Lamb

EXAMPLES

 American Brett

 Belgian-Style Flanders

INTERACTIONS

Combining these flavors brings out
umami and adds earthy notes that
rest on the center of the palate.

Example Dish: Grilled rib eye and root vegetables

FOOD COMPONENT
GAME BIRDS & GRAINS

BEER FLAVORS
HOPPY & BITTER

EXAMPLES

- Duck
- Quail
- Quinoa
- Farro

EXAMPLES

American Pale Ale

American Brown Ale

INTERACTIONS

Complements roastiness
(Maillard reaction) while fat
neutralizes hop bitterness.

Example Dish: Roasted quail with farrotto

FOOD COMPONENT
FATS

EXAMPLES

- Butter
- Olive oil
- Duck/pork fat
- Dairy

BEER FLAVORS
HOPPY & BITTER, DARK & ROASTY

EXAMPLES

American Black Ale

English-Style Brown Porter

INTERACTIONS

Beer cuts through fat, balances
strong flavors, and allows for a
complex finish.

Example Dish: Cashew butter and red pepper jelly on toast

FOOD COMPONENT
VEGETABLES (GRILLED)

BEER FLAVORS
DARK & ROASTY

EXAMPLES

- Carrots
- Mild peppers
- Onions
- Mushrooms

EXAMPLES

Irish-Style Dry Stout

German-Style Schwarzbier

INTERACTIONS

Brings out umami and balances
sweetness and richness.

Example Dish: Green chili-stuffed portobello

FOOD COMPONENT
CHEESE

BEER FLAVORS
VARIES

EXAMPLES

- Brie (Fruity & Spicy)
- Gouda (Malty & Sweet)
- Aged cheddar (Hoppy & Bitter)

EXAMPLES

 Belgian-Style Tripel

 English-Style Pale Ale

INTERACTIONS

Beer complements the natural flavors and textures while cutting through fat, cleansing the palate.

Example Dish: Brie and fruit

FOOD COMPONENT
BRAISED MEATS & CHOCOLATE

BEER FLAVORS
MALTY & SWEET, DARK & ROASTY

EXAMPLES

- Beef short ribs
- Pork shoulder

- <50% cacao
  (Malty & Sweet)
- >55% cacao
  (Dark & Roasty)

EXAMPLES

 German-Style Bock

 Baltic-Style Porter

INTERACTIONS

Highlights the roasted character
(Maillard reaction).

Example Dish: Milk chocolate bread pudding

PORK

HOPPY & BITTER, FRUITY & SWEET

EXAMPLES

- Sausage
- Tenderloin
- Terrine

EXAMPLES

  Imperial IPA

  Belgian-Style Dubbel

INTERACTIONS

The intensity of the pork fat stands
up to the strong beer characteristics.

Example Dish: Pork chops and apple relish

FOOD COMPONENT	BEER FLAVORS
CREAMY DESSERTS	**VARIES**

EXAMPLES

- Cheesecake
- Ice cream
- Crème brûlée
- Mousse cake

EXAMPLES

 British-Style Barleywine

 Belgian-Style Fruit Lambic

INTERACTIONS

Balances richness on the palate so
the dessert doesn't finish cloyingly.

Example Dish: Butterscotch mousse with dark chocolate

CRAFT BEER AND CHEESE

INTERACTIONS

Cheese is a challenging one-ingredient dish to match with most beverages. The variety of pungent, strong, earthy, and creamy flavors of cheese can confuse the palate. Craft beer, however, has flavor profiles that often mirror artisan cheeses and pairing can enhance the flavors of both the beer and cheese.

Cheese and craft beer both benefit from proper serving temperatures. Let cheese warm from cold storage to a temperature of around 55–60°F.

Delicate craft beers often pair well with young cheeses, while stronger flavored craft beers tend to work better with strongly flavored, mature cheeses. Look for commonalities (e.g., malt-forward craft beers pair with nutty or sweet cheeses) and contrasting interactions (e.g., hop-forward bitter beers cut through fatty richness). Recognize complementary sensations and interactions in the pairing; hop-intense craft beers pair well with acidic or salty cheeses. Arrange pairing order from least intense to most intense flavors. Avoid commingling cheeses and use separate utensils for each.

STYLE GUIDE

List of cheese styles adapted from "Cheese Definitions and Categories," American Cheese Society (website), https://www.cheesesociety.org/events-education/cheese-definitions/. Beer styles and descriptions provided by the author.

FRESH CHEESE

The term *fresh* is used to describe cheeses that have not been aged or are very slightly cured. These cheeses have a high moisture content, are usually mild, and have a very creamy taste and soft texture.

These light cheeses pair excellently with the softer flavors of wheat and lambic beers.

. . . .

EXAMPLES

- Italian-style mascarpone and ricotta

- Chèvre

- Feta

- Cream cheese

- Quark

- Cottage cheese

. . . .

BEER PAIRING STYLES

- Wheat Beer

- Belgian-Style Lambic/Gueuze

SEMI-SOFT CHEESE

Semi-soft cheeses have little to no rind and exhibit a smooth, generally creamy interior. These cheeses have a wide range of flavors, from mild to rather pungent in taste.

The vast variety of cheeses in this category means they can be paired with many different craft beers. When pairing, remember to match strength with strength.

EXAMPLES

- Blue cheeses
- Colby
- Fontina styles
- Havarti
- Monterey Jack

BEER PAIRING STYLES

- Varies

FIRM/HARD CHEESE

Firm/hard cheeses form a broad category of cheeses that range from very mild to sharp and pungent. The texture profiles are equally wide-ranging, with some that are elastic at room temperature to hard grating cheeses that can be difficult to cut.

Because of their variety, hard cheeses are easily paired with an equally broad range of craft beer styles.

EXAMPLES

- Varies

BEER PAIRING STYLES

- Pilsner and Pale Lager
- Bock
- Brown Ale
- American Imperial Stout

BLUE CHEESE

The term *blue* is used to describe cheeses that have distinctive blue/green veining, created when the *Penicillium roqueforti* mold, which is added during the cheesemaking process, is exposed to air. This mold provides a distinct flavor to the cheese, which ranges from fairly mild to assertive and pungent.

These strongly flavored cheeses are most successfully paired with stronger-flavored, bolder beers.

EXAMPLES

- French (Roquefort)
- Italian (Gorgonzola)
- Danish blue

BEER PAIRING STYLES

- India Pale Ale
- Imperial IPA

NATURAL RIND CHEESE

Natural-rind cheeses develop rinds naturally during aging. This category of cheeses includes Tomme de Savoie styles, which pair well with golden ales or blonde ales. Traditional British-style ales work well with English-style natural rind cheeses, such as Lancashire and Stilton.

EXAMPLES

- Tomme de Savoie
- Lancashire
- Stilton

BEER PAIRING STYLES

- Belgian-Style Golden Strong Ale
- Blonde Ale
- English-Style Bitter

WASHED-RIND CHEESE

Washed-rind cheeses are bathed in brine, wine, spirits, or even beer, which helps the cheese to retain moisture and aids the growth of bacteria.

The cheese itself, while potentially pungent, is often creamy. Try Belgian-styles ales like tripels and golden strong ales with these varieties of cheese.

EXAMPLES

- Jasper Hill Farm (Winnimere)
- Chimay (Beer Washed)
- Twig Farm (Washed Wheel)

BEER PAIRING STYLES

- Belgian-Style Tripel
- Belgian-Style Golden Strong Ale

TASTING LOG

CRAFT BEER CAN BE AN ADVENTURE.

As you experiment along the way, log your thoughts to keep track of which beers you liked and watch your palate develop over time.

BEER NAME:

Brewery:

Style:

IBU: ABV: Date:

Notes:

BEER NAME:

Brewery:

Style:

IBU: ABV: Date:

Notes:

BEER NAME:

Brewery:

Style:

IBU: ABV: Date:

Notes:

BEER NAME:

Brewery:

Style:

IBU: ABV: Date:

Notes:

BEER NAME:

Brewery:

Style:

IBU: ABV: Date:

Notes:

BEER NAME: ....

Brewery: ....

Style: ....

IBU: .... ABV: .... Date: ....

Notes: ....

....

BEER NAME: ....

Brewery: ....

Style: ....

IBU: .... ABV: .... Date: ....

Notes: ....

....

BEER NAME: ....

Brewery: ....

Style: ....

IBU: .... ABV: .... Date: ....

Notes: ....

....

BEER NAME: ....

Brewery: ....

Style: ....

IBU: .... ABV: .... Date: ....

Notes: ....

....

BEER NAME: ....

Brewery: ....

Style: ....

IBU: .... ABV: .... Date: ....

Notes: ....

....

BEER NAME: ....

Brewery: ....

Style: ....

IBU: .... ABV: .... Date: ....

Notes: ....

....

BEER NAME:

Brewery:

Style:

IBU: ABV: Date:

Notes:

BEER NAME:

Brewery:

Style:

IBU: ABV: Date:

Notes:

BEER NAME:

Brewery:

Style:

IBU: ABV: Date:

Notes:

BEER NAME:

Brewery:

Style:

IBU: .... ABV: .... Date: ....

Notes:

BEER NAME:

Brewery:

Style:

IBU: .... ABV: .... Date: ....

Notes:

BEER NAME:

Brewery:

Style:

IBU: .... ABV: .... Date: ....

Notes:

BEER NAME:

Brewery:

Style:

IBU: ABV: Date:

Notes:

BEER NAME:

Brewery:

Style:

IBU: ABV: Date:

Notes:

BEER NAME:

Brewery:

Style:

IBU: ABV: Date:

Notes:

BEER NAME:

Brewery:

Style:

IBU: ABV: Date:

Notes:

BEER NAME:

Brewery:

Style:

IBU: ABV: Date:

Notes:

BEER NAME:

Brewery:

Style:

IBU: ABV: Date:

Notes:

BEER NAME:

Brewery:

Style:

IBU: ABV: Date:

Notes:

BEER NAME:

Brewery:

Style:

IBU: ABV: Date:

Notes:

BEER NAME:

Brewery:

Style:

IBU: ABV: Date:

Notes:

BEER NAME:

Brewery:

Style:

IBU: ABV: Date:

Notes:

BEER NAME:

Brewery:

Style:

IBU: ABV: Date:

Notes:

BEER NAME:

Brewery:

Style:

IBU: ABV: Date:

Notes:

BEER NAME: ....

Brewery: ....

Style: ....

IBU: .... ABV: .... Date: ....

Notes: ....

....

BEER NAME: ....

Brewery: ....

Style: ....

IBU: .... ABV: .... Date: ....

Notes: ....

....

BEER NAME: ....

Brewery: ....

Style: ....

IBU: .... ABV: .... Date: ....

Notes: ....

....

BEER NAME: ....

Brewery: ....

Style: ....

IBU: ....   ABV: ....   Date: ....

Notes: ....

....

BEER NAME: ....

Brewery: ....

Style: ....

IBU: ....   ABV: ....   Date: ....

Notes: ....

....

BEER NAME: ....

Brewery: ....

Style: ....

IBU: ....   ABV: ....   Date: ....

Notes: ....

....

BEER NAME: ....

Brewery: ....

Style: ....

IBU: .... ABV: .... Date: ....

Notes: ....

....

BEER NAME: ....

Brewery: ....

Style: ....

IBU: .... ABV: .... Date: ....

Notes: ....

....

BEER NAME: ....

Brewery: ....

Style: ....

IBU: .... ABV: .... Date: ....

Notes: ....

....

BEER NAME:

Brewery:

Style:

IBU: .... ABV: .... Date:

Notes:

BEER NAME:

Brewery:

Style:

IBU: .... ABV: .... Date:

Notes:

BEER NAME:

Brewery:

Style:

IBU: .... ABV: .... Date:

Notes:

BEER NAME:

Brewery:

Style:

IBU: ABV: Date:

Notes:

BEER NAME:

Brewery:

Style:

IBU: ABV: Date:

Notes:

BEER NAME:

Brewery:

Style:

IBU: ABV: Date:

Notes:

BEER NAME:

Brewery:

Style:

IBU: ABV: Date:

Notes:

BEER NAME:

Brewery:

Style:

IBU: ABV: Date:

Notes:

BEER NAME:

Brewery:

Style:

IBU: ABV: Date:

Notes:

BEER NAME:

Brewery:

Style:

IBU: .... ABV: .... Date:

Notes:

BEER NAME:

Brewery:

Style:

IBU: .... ABV: .... Date:

Notes:

BEER NAME:

Brewery:

Style:

IBU: .... ABV: .... Date:

Notes:

BEER NAME:

Brewery:

Style:

IBU: ABV: Date:

Notes:

BEER NAME:

Brewery:

Style:

IBU: ABV: Date:

Notes:

BEER NAME:

Brewery:

Style:

IBU: ABV: Date:

Notes:

BEER NAME:

Brewery:

Style:

IBU: ABV: Date:

Notes:

BEER NAME:

Brewery:

Style:

IBU: ABV: Date:

Notes:

BEER NAME:

Brewery:

Style:

IBU: ABV: Date:

Notes:

BEER NAME: ....

Brewery: ....

Style: ....

IBU: .... ABV: .... Date: ....

Notes: ....

....

BEER NAME: ....

Brewery: ....

Style: ....

IBU: .... ABV: .... Date: ....

Notes: ....

....

BEER NAME: ....

Brewery: ....

Style: ....

IBU: .... ABV: .... Date: ....

Notes: ....

....

BEER NAME: ....

Brewery: ....

Style: ....

IBU: .... ABV: .... Date: ....

Notes: ....

....

BEER NAME: ....

Brewery: ....

Style: ....

IBU: .... ABV: .... Date: ....

Notes: ....

....

BEER NAME: ....

Brewery: ....

Style: ....

IBU: .... ABV: .... Date: ....

Notes: ....

....

BEER NAME: ....

Brewery: ....

Style: ....

IBU: .... ABV: .... Date: ....

Notes: ....

....

BEER NAME: ....

Brewery: ....

Style: ....

IBU: .... ABV: .... Date: ....

Notes: ....

....

BEER NAME: ....

Brewery: ....

Style: ....

IBU: .... ABV: .... Date: ....

Notes: ....

....

BEER NAME: ....

Brewery: ....

Style: ....

IBU: .... ABV: .... Date: ....

Notes: ....

....

BEER NAME: ....

Brewery: ....

Style: ....

IBU: .... ABV: .... Date: ....

Notes: ....

....

BEER NAME: ....

Brewery: ....

Style: ....

IBU: .... ABV: .... Date: ....

Notes: ....

....

BEER NAME: ....

Brewery: ....

Style: ....

IBU: .... ABV: .... Date: ....

Notes: ....

....

BEER NAME: ....

Brewery: ....

Style: ....

IBU: .... ABV: .... Date: ....

Notes: ....

....

BEER NAME: ....

Brewery: ....

Style: ....

IBU: .... ABV: .... Date: ....

Notes: ....

....

BEER NAME: ....

Brewery: ....

Style: ....

IBU: .... ABV: .... Date: ....

Notes: ....

....

BEER NAME: ....

Brewery: ....

Style: ....

IBU: .... ABV: .... Date: ....

Notes: ....

....

BEER NAME: ....

Brewery: ....

Style: ....

IBU: .... ABV: .... Date: ....

Notes: ....

....

BEER NAME:

Brewery:

Style:

IBU: ABV: Date:

Notes:

BEER NAME:

Brewery:

Style:

IBU: ABV: Date:

Notes:

BEER NAME:

Brewery:

Style:

IBU: ABV: Date:

Notes:

INDEX